THE AMERICAN SOLUTION

ORIGINS OF THE UNITED STATES CONSTITUTION

Robert A. Rutland

Library of Congress

Washington

1987

Cover: "Back of the State House, Philadelphia" (detail). From William Birch, *The City of Philadelphia*, 1800.
Rare Book and Special Collections Division

Inside cover: "Plan of the City and Environs of Philadelphia," with an elevation of the State House. Engraved by William Faden, 1777.
Geography and Map Division

This book has been published in conjunction with a major exhibition of the same name held at the Library of Congress, May 14 through September 17, 1987, and as part of the Library's celebration of the bicentennial of the U.S. Constitution. Most of the items illustrated here were assembled for the exhibition, primarily from the Library's own collections, but also from a number of other institutions. They were selected for the publication by John R. Sellers, curator of the exhibition.

Library of Congress Cataloging-in-Publication Data

Rutland, Robert Allen, 1922–
    The American solution.
    "Published in conjunction with a major exhibition of the same name held at the Library of Congress, May 14 through September 17, 1987"—T.p. verso.
    Bibliography: p.
    Supt. of Docs. no. : LC 1.2:Am3/13
    1. United States—Constitutional history.
2. United States. Constitutional Convention (1787)
I. Title.
KF4541.R79 1987   342.73'029   86-607919
ISBN 0-8444-0547-7   347.30229

For sale by the Superintendent of Documents,
U.S. Government Printing Office,
Washington, D. C. 20402

Contents

The great desideratum in Government is, so to modify the sovereignty as that it may be sufficiently neutral between different parts of the Society to controul one part from invading the rights of another, and at the same time sufficiently controuled itself, from setting up an interest adverse to that of the entire Society.

James Madison to Thomas Jefferson, October 1787

A. N.W. VIEW OF THE STATE HOUSE IN PHILADELPHIA *taken* 1778

"A N.W. View of the State House in Philadelphia taken 1778." Engraving by James Thackara from the *Columbia Magazine*, July 1787. *Prints and Photographs Division*

Was the Revolution a Blessing or a Curse?

The highroad to Philadelphia for the Constitutional Convention of 1787 began in western Massachusetts a year earlier when a band of penurious farmers decided to take the law into their own hands. No one could have foreseen that the musket fire rattling near Springfield would reverberate in the coffeehouses of New York and Boston, the parlor of Mount Vernon, or the American ministry in Paris. While the reactions varied, the fracas started by the embattled Yankee farmers in the summer of 1786—which came to be known as Shays's Rebellion—galvanized the movers and shakers of the new nation into action. "For God's sake tell me what is the cause of all these commotions?" Washington thundered when he heard of the outbreak. The story of how the Constitution of the United States came into being is essentially one of frustration and misunderstanding, but it has a happy long-range outcome.

The plight of the Massachusetts farmers three years after the American Revolution ended was only a local form of the mounting national malaise. The Treaty of Paris, signed in 1783, ended eight years of sporadic warfare. As Washington prepared to leave the army, he issued a veiled warning to the new nation:

It appears to me there is an option still left to the United States of America. . . . According to the system of Policy the States shall adopt at this moment, they will stand or fall, and . . . it is yet to be decided, whether the Revolution must ultimately be considered a blessing or a curse: a blessing or a curse, not to the present age alone, for with our fate will the destiny of unborn Millions be involved.

Washington sent his plea for "A Sacred regard to Public Justice" to the thirteen

Intelligence relating to Insurgents — Dec. 1786

8th a little after five P.M. — this afternoon Mr. R. told me that Dr. Sloss in coming out of Boston met Mr. Dix of Worcester going in, who told Dr. S. that he had left Worcester late on the evening of the 7th. Insurgents about 600, disheartened, & talk of proposing terms of surrender. Dix that 600 large measure).

One Ses̄t of Sturbridge, I am since told (a faithful citizen) came through Worcester last evening. He told me that some of the Insurgents who belonged to the neighboring towns had gone home, & others quartered with them. That he was informed that about ten minutes before he got into Wor. a party of 1000 men had gone out towards Holden. He says report varies with regard to the whole number from a few hundreds to 13,000. His own opinion was that they were about twenty five hundred

At half past eight Mr. W— informed me that he had spent the evening at the Anchor with a traveller from the N. Parish in Brookfield, who told him that he was going to Portsmouth, & came through Worcester at dusk last evening. The traveller at first appeared cautious, but by degrees grew more communicative. He said that not one insurgent came out of Brookfield; the inhabitants in general not disposed to act either way; however a party of 40 men marched as militia from the Mr. Fiske's parish to defend the Court, & had got as far as Spencer when the storm came on last monday evening & prevented their progress. When he entered Worcester last evening he found Shays's men drawn up, four deep, & extending in the Street from Nazro's corner to Brown's, nearly equal to one side of W. common, supposed to be about 900 yards, in order for marching over to Paxton where they were to be billeted on the inhabitants. He learned that Wheeler had a little before marched his men over to Holden where they were to be quartered. There was no talk of disbanding, but they said a large body was on the way down from Berkshire with a drove of cattle. The army at Worcester subsisted this week on their own provisions. The report was that they were about sending to the neighboring towns for their concurrence in a petition, to suspend all courts of common pleas till after the next election, & to liberate Shattuck & his fellow prisoners. The traveller was found to be Brigham a trader in Brookfield. He supposes the address of the Court will not produce any effect on the insurgents, but is much admired by the faithful.

9th a severe snow storm prevents all communication this day. Col. Crafts's son, of Sturbridge, informs me that his father's regiment of horse is nearly completed, several companies being quite filled.

"Intelligence relating to Insurgents," December 1786. *Manuscript Division*

The insurrection in western Massachusetts led by Daniel Shays was commonly reported in newspapers and private letters. But this secret account by an unknown author is more indicative of the serious interpretation many Americans attached to the event.

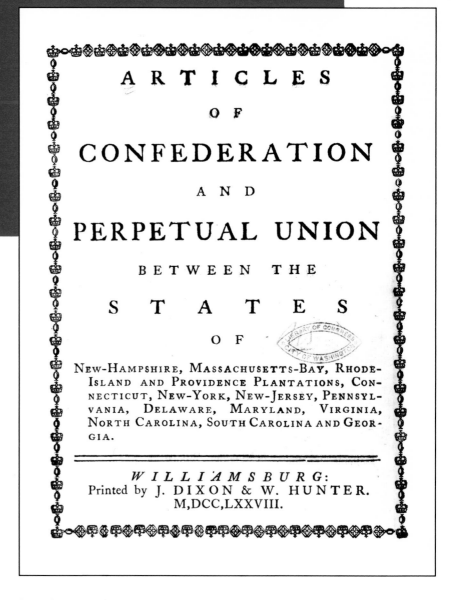

governors, hoping they would spread his message to state legislators. At the outset, a postwar boom focused attention on the economy rather than governmental
policy, as the long pent-up demand for goods (particularly British imports) created
an illusion of prosperity. Much of the trading was done on credit, however, and
eventually the merchants and bankers wanted cash. By 1785 the joy of a victory
over England had faded, to be followed by sober realities in the marketplace, in

Mr Johnson

An ADDRES from the UNITED STATES in CONGRESS assembled, to the LEGISLATURES of the several STATES.

WHEN the interests of a people are endangered, either through the defect of the government they have established, or the want of timely and vigorous exertions to give efficacy to its operations, it becomes the duty of those to whom the sacred trust of watching over the welfare of the nation is delegated, to awaken it to a sense of its danger, and to urge the adoption of such measures, as may avert the calamities with which it is threatened.

Impressed with a sense of this high obligation, and an anxious and affectionate concern for the interest, honour and safety of their constituents, the United States in Congress assembled, have, at various periods, and on various occasions, exercised this important trust; but on none more solemn and interesting, than on the 18th February last, when after a mature and serious consideration of the state of the nation, they were constrained to declare,—"That a reliance on the requisitions to discharge the engagements of the confederacy, would be dangerous to the welfare and peace of the union: That for want of a timely exertion in establishing a general revenue, not only the existence of the confederacy was hazarded, but those great and invaluable privileges for which they had contended; and therefore that, whilst Congress were denied the means of satisfying these engagements, which they had constitutionally entered into for the common benefit of the union, it was their duty to warn their constituents that the most fatal evils would inevitably flow from a breach of public faith, pledged by solemn contract, and a violation of those principles of justice which are the only solid basis of the honour and prosperity of nations."

It would be unnecessary on this occasion to recapitulate the reasons which induced the recommendation of the revenue system of the 18th April, 1783. The necessity of a compliance with the general impost (which constituted a principal part of this system) and the benefits or evils which would inevitably flow from a neglect or adoption of the measure, are so forcibly pointed out in the act of Congress of the 16th December, 1782, (which accompanied their address of the 18th April, 1783, and by their subsequent resolves of the 18th February last, that nothing can be added to enforce the policy and necessity of the measure; unless it be this solemn and lamentable truth,—that the experience of the last year has added further proof of the utter inefficacy of relying upon requisitions for supporting the expence and credit of the union.

By this requisition the states were called upon to pay into the general treasury, on or before the first day of May last, the sum of three million of dollars, of which one million of dollars was to be discharged by specie, and two million of dollars by discounts of interest on the domestic debt. The objects for which the monies proposed to be raised were to be appropriated, are distinctly pointed out. By this it appears that the sum of eight hundred and forty thousand dollars, were absolutely and indispensibly necessary to be paid some months since in specie, to defray the charges of the civil government, and the interest of the foreign debt.

What have been the effects of this requisition? Notwithstanding the serious and interesting appeal of Congress to the justice and wisdom of the several states, which soon followed it; and in which, after stating the public receipts and expenditures for the four preceding years, it is proved that the receipts of the last fourteen months, were not adequate to the bare maintenance of the federal government, on the most economical establishment, and in time of profound peace: Only eight states out of the thirteen have passed acts apparently complying with the requisition; and by such as have complied, not more than the sum of 100,000 dollars has been paid into the general treasury to the present date, in actual specie.

In examining the acts of the several legislatures, passed in consequence of the resolves of the 27th September last, it is found that in most states, the monies intended for the purposes of the union, and those of the state, are blended in the same collection; that scarcely in any state, funds are pointed out by the law for providing its quota; and that in several, a paper currency is made receivable as specie in all payments whatsoever. To these, amongst other circumstances, may be imputed in a great degree, the inefficacy of the revenue laws in the several states, and an almost total stagnation in the payment of the general quotas.

If it be asked, to what end then is another requisition made, whilst such heavy balances remain still unsatisfied? The answer is, That the United States in Congress are bound by every principle of good faith and justice, and a regard to national character, to exercise that authority (however inadequate) which is vested in them, for obliging the different members of the union to contribute their respective quotas for the support of the general government; and to manifest to the world, that they are not unworthy the high and honourable trust of watching over the welfare of a free people.

The states will observe that in the present requisition, no less than 1,723,626 dollars 47-90ths, ought to be forthwith raised in specie, for the express purpose of paying the interest, and certain installments of principal of the foreign debt, which will become due in the present, and in the course of

Henry Knox. Portrait by
Gilbert Stuart.
*Photograph in Prints and
Photographs Division*

A Revolutionary War officer
and future secretary of war,
Henry Knox was deeply concerned about the state of the
nation and kept George Washington informed about Shays's
Rebellion. He urged Washington to accept the invitation to
serve as a delegate to the Constitutional Convention.

the legislative hall, and on the farms and plantations that provided most Americans with their livelihood. Thoughtful Americans began to perceive that by leaving the British Empire they had not altogether solved their problems. The postwar letdown in the thirteen United States was probably more psychological than real, in that people found their cupboards as full as in prewar days. But their cashboxes were not, and the promised prosperity that made wartime sacrifices easier was short-lived.

Recall the circumstances that brought on the war for independence: taxes had been the central, exacerbating issue. Led by lawyers and a small force of planter-patriots, Americans were persuaded that the payment of taxes without representation violated their fundamental rights as American-born Englishmen. Resistance to such abuse was initially popular and fashionable, then patriotic, and finally a fixed, militant policy. Once there was peace, however, most citizens stuck with their old convictions about taxes—the fewer (or none) the better—and aspiring state politicians were reluctant to cross their constituents. In town meetings, at county courthouses, or wherever Americans congregated (in churchyards, taverns, or public houses) the talk was blunt. That Americans were among the least-taxed people in Christendom mattered not a whit.

At the national level, there was another problem. The weakness of the Articles of Confederation, patched together for the war but inadequate for the peace, came home to roost by 1785. No longer could printing presses issue Continental currency—the dollars were hardly worth the paper they were printed on—and once the overhanging British threat vanished nimble wartime financial arrangements collapsed. Winning the war had cost over $70 million in debt, interest payments were either far in arrears or ignored, and the national treasury was a shambles. Most states ignored their obligation to send their quota of cash to the Continental treasurer, and in some cases they flooded the market with depreciated currency that forced silver and gold coins out of sight. In short, the United States tottered on the brink of bankruptcy.

An empty national treasury was bad enough, but worse still was the indifference of leading state politicians to the new republic's financial crisis. No citizen read the signs as carefully as George Washington. Officially retired and seemingly settled into plantation routine, Washington could not follow the flow of events without feelings of anger. News of the Shays outbreak in September 1786 upset Washington so much he had difficulty in controlling his reaction.

I am mortified beyond expression when I view the clouds that have spread over the brightest morn that ever dawned upon any Country. In a word, I am lost in amazement when I behold what intrigue, the interested views of desperate characters, ignorance and jealousy of the minor part, are capable of effecting, as a scourge on the major part of our fellow Citizens of the Union.[1]

How strange! How sad! Unburdening his thoughts to "Lighthorse Harry" Lee, Washington told his former comrade-in-arms that "the present tumults in Massachusetts" called for more than a signal from him. Lee had suggested that Washington exert his influence to quell the disturbance. In the first place, Washington said, he doubted that influence "would be a proper remedy for the disorders." More to the point, "Influence is no Government. Let us have one by which our lives, liberties and properties will be secured; or let us know the worst at once."

Washington's reaction to the Shays uprising was to become the vital ingredient in the reform movement of 1786. Indeed, it is not an overstatement to say that had there been no Shays's Rebellion, a dramatic impetus behind the movement for a new constitution would have been lacking. In the same way that Pearl Harbor crystallized public opinion in 1941, the Shays outbreak forced citizens in 1786 to realize the dimensions of the nation's crisis.

One of Washington's great qualities was his ability to see a situation in the same light as the average citizen. Thus there was great perception in Washington's sense of outrage that Americans were now training their gunsights on other Americans. Here was "melancholy proof of what our trans-Atlantic foe has predicted," for it was well-known that in England the Tories expected an American collapse. In 1786 at a London dinner party Jefferson sat next to a general, "a Scotchman and ministerialist," who warned him "that were America to petition parliament to be again received on their former footing, the petition would be very generally rejected." "I think it was the sentiment of the company, and is the sentiment perhaps of the nation," Jefferson reported. Maybe the bad news from Massachusetts proved the Englishmen were right.

Neither Washington nor his informants were sympathetic to the farmers who defied tax-collectors, for Shays and his followers had defied the law; and for all

their instincts of fairness toward others who lived off the fruits of the earth, citizens who thought like Washington exalted the law above livelihood. (This seemed to be the one English trait Americans had retained as they forsook others.) The inarticulate yeomen saw their farms jeopardized and their livestock auctioned for back taxes, and grabbed their rifles in frustration. Boston-based efforts to squelch the rebellion were applauded, while newspapers ignored the causes of the outbreaks. Even Henry Knox, who helped whip up Washington's indignation, admitted that the insurgent farmers never numbered over twelve hundred, and hundreds carried

Thomas Jefferson. Portrait by
Charles Willson Peale.
Photograph in Prints and Photographs Division

From his post in Paris as
ambassador to France,
Jefferson exchanged letters
with his old friend James
Madison during the summer of
1787 and kept abreast of the
progress of the convention.

only farm implements or clubs for lack of a gun. To defeat this primitive force, a militia of over four thousand marched westward and quickly dispersed the pitiful protesters. By February 1787 the Shays business was over, but the shouting lingered on in high places.

The upstart farmers provided a convenient handle for those patriots of '76 who looked upon the American Revolution as a godsend to mankind. Granted that mistakes had been made, to these men (who would be known to history as "the Founding Fathers") nothing could diminish the luster of the supreme accomplishment of fighting England and winning independence. For Washington, Franklin, Jefferson, Madison, and Adams there were plenty of small differences of opinion, but they could all agree that (to answer Washington's rhetorical question) the Revolution had been a blessing. This shared feeling of accomplishment was blighted, of course, by postwar events. The confederation shrank toward impotence as the Continental Congress was poorly attended and capable of furnishing nothing more than recommendations or requisitions. By 1786 it was a paper government depending upon handouts, which was no government at all. Woefully short on leadership and money, Congress went through the motions of governing, while the country's financial structure verged on collapse. The nadir of American fortunes was reached late in 1786 when rumors circulated in New England that important men were planning meetings "for the purpose of reuniting the American States to the Government of Great Britain." Perhaps Jefferson's dinner companion was right.[2]

Adversity makes some men cowards while it brings out the firmest qualities in others. The suggestion that America ought to abandon its experiment in self-government and crawl back into the English fold as a repentant failure made dedicated Americans bristle. Foremost among the public men who viewed the events in Massachusetts with alarm but not horror was James Madison. When his friend Thomas Jefferson heard of the Shays uprising and commented that he was not disturbed, for "a little rebellion now and then is a good thing," Madison may have agreed in one sense. *This* rebellion was leading intelligent citizens to determine on a course of action that would turn the country around. Thus Madison saw in the clamor for a stronger or at least a sterner government an opportunity long lacking in American councils. Unquestionably the Shays incident gave reform-minded citizens, with Madison in the foreground, an excuse to raise the alarm that culminated in the Federal Convention of 1787.

Madison was well qualified to look at postwar America with the eye of a diagnosing physician. Since 1776 he had been involved in the Revolution, either as a state legislator or in the Continental Congress (where he earned a solid reputation for hard work and clear understanding of the nation's problems). Whether he sought a stiff measure assuring freedom of religion or a tough policy against Spain regarding use of the Mississippi River, Madison consistently approached each difficulty with sound reasoning. Ultimately, Madison concluded that the new republic could not survive unless a workable taxing program could be forced upon those recalcitrant state politicians who jealously defended their low-or-no tax plans. Beyond the matter of revenues and payments on the wartime debts lay the other major matter of external commerce, which was left to each state to control. Only jealousy and bickering resulted from this oversight in the Articles of Confederation; and early in 1786 a congressional committee confessed that "the want of power in Congress to form a system regulatory of foreign commerce" threatens "the union . . . with annihilation."[3]

Madison's decision that the Articles of Confederation had outlived their usefulness coincided with Shays's Rebellion. To Madison, as to Washington, this was the last straw. Early in 1785, and in violation of the Articles, delegates from Virginia and Maryland had convened at Mount Vernon to discuss outstanding problems, and the resulting compact provided a start in the direction toward reform. With some trepidation, Madison represented Virginia at the abortive Annapolis convention in September 1786. Although skeptical that anything worthwhile would emerge from the Maryland gathering, Madison believed any "idea of bracing the federal system" was "better than nothing."

Predictably, the problems of the Confederation evoked much breast-beating but no real action. (Maryland itself failed to send a delegation!) The Shays turmoil, the poor attendance at Annapolis, and the dismal reports of a widespread farm depression hardened Madison's resolve. Madison realized there was no hope for the nation unless the Articles were abandoned, and his conversations in the Maryland capital with fellow delegate Alexander Hamilton may have reinforced this apprehension.

Hamilton traveled from New York for the Annapolis meeting and would have returned in a petulant mood if he had not found a common ground with Madison. Even more than the Virginian, Hamilton was disgusted with the dilatory state

1. Front View of the State-House &c. at ANNAPOLIS the Capital of MARYLAND.

governments, and since 1783 both men had urged enactment of a national tax program that would avert financial disaster. Madison's proposal for "the establishment of permanent & adequate funds to operate generally throughout the U. States" was rejected by the states, leading to three years of drifting while an atmosphere of crisis mounted. In these circumstances Hamilton must have told Madison in Annapolis that he would do what he could to persuade sound-thinking New Yorkers that drastic reforms alone would save the republic.

While public hysteria over the Shays incident mounted, Madison returned to Virginia and worked behind the scenes in the state legislature to promote a national meeting in Philadelphia on the following May "for the Purpose of revising the fœderal Constitution."[4] With the blessing of Congress and without much argument elsewhere the invitation was issued to all the states, and Virginia appointed to her delegation George Washington, Patrick Henry (who declined), Madison, Dr. James McClurg, George Mason, Governor Edmund Randolph, George Wythe, and John

The Maryland State House at Annapolis.
Engraving by John Vallance from the *Columbia Magazine*, February 1789

The Philadelphia convention would never have been called if the Annapolis meeting of 1786 had succeeded in solving the financial problems the United States faced after the Revolution. Poor attendance made a second gathering necessary, and Congress responded to the recommendation of the Annapolis delegates by calling on all states to send delegates to Philadelphia in May 1787.

AN ACT

FOR APPOINTING DEPUTIES FROM THIS COMMONWEALTH TO A CONVENTION
PROPOSED TO BE HELD IN THE CITY OF PHILADELPHIA IN MAY NEXT, FOR
THE PURPOSE OF REVISING THE FŒDERAL CONSTITUTION.

WHEREAS the Commissioners who assembled at Annapolis, on the fourteenth of September last, for the purpose of devising and reporting the means of enabling Congress to provide effectually for the Commercial Interest of the United States, have represented the necessity of extending the revision of the fœderal system to all its defects; and have recommended, that Deputies for that purpose be appointed by the several Legislatures to meet in convention in the city of Philadelphia, on the second day of May next; a provision which seems preferable to a discussion of the subject in Congress, where it might be too much interrupted by the ordinary business before them; and where it would besides, be deprived of the valuable councils of sundry individuals, who are disqualified by the constitution or laws of particular states, or restrained by peculiar circumstances from a seat in that Assembly:

AND WHEREAS, the General Assembly of this Commonwealth, taking into view the actual situation of the Confederacy, as well as reflecting on the alarming representations made from time to time, by the United States in Congress, particularly in their act of the fifteenth day of February last, can no longer doubt that the crisis is arrived at which the good people of America are to decide the solemn question, whether they will by wise and magnanimous efforts reap the just fruits of that independance which they have so gloriously acquired, and of that Union which they have cemented with so much of their common blood; or whether, by giving way to unmanly jealousies and prejudices, or to partial and transitory interests, they will renounce the auspicious blessings prepared for them by the Revolution, and furnish to its enemies an eventual triumph over those, by whose virtue and valour, it has been accomplished:

AND WHEREAS, the same noble and extended Policy, and the same fraternal and affectionate sentiments, which originally determined the Citizens of this Commonwealth, to unite with their Brethren of the other States, in establishing a fœderal Government, cannot but be felt with equal force now as the motives to lay aside every inferior consideration, and to concur in such farther concessions and provisions, as may be necessary to secure the great objects for which that Government was instituted, and to render the United States as happy in Peace, as they have been glorious in war.

Be it therefore enacted, by the General Assembly of the Commonwealth of Virginia, That seven Commissioners be appointed by joint ballot of both Houses of Assembly, who, or any three of them, are hereby authorized as Deputies from this Commonwealth to meet such Deputies as may be appointed and authorized by other states, to assemble in Convention at Philadelphia, as above recommended, and to join with them in devising and discussing all such alterations and farther provisions, as may be necessary to render the fœderal Constitution, adequate to the exigencies of the Union, and in reporting such an act for that purpose, to the United States in Congress, as when agreed to by them, and duly confirmed by the several states, will effectually provide for the same.

And be it further enacted, That in case of the death of any of the said Deputies, or of their declining their appointments, the Executive are hereby authorized to supply such vacancies; and the Governor is requested to transmit forthwith a copy of this Act, to the United States in Congress, and to the Executives of each of the states in the Union.

November 9, 1786, read the third time and passed the House of Delegates.

JOHN BECKLEY, c. H. D.

November 23, 1786, passed the Senate.

H. BROOKE, c. s.

"An Act for Appointing Deputies . . .," November 23, 1786. *Manuscript Division*

Without the inspiring presence of George Washington, the Philadelphia convention might have ended in frustration and inaction. Virginia's appointment of Washington to the state's delegation ensured the attendance of talented men from all over the Union.

14

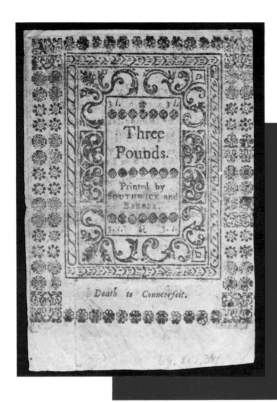

Blair. This was no ordinary group of men. The mere publication of their names in newspapers told readers that the delegation meant business.

Now the fat was in the fire, for Madison never dreamed of working merely to amend the Articles of Confederation. He wanted a new start at the business of saving the American Union. And Madison saw that he must depend on Washington's fame to provide the spark that would keep the embers of the American Revolution alive.

If there had been no Shays uprising, Washington might have made excuses and stayed off the Virginia delegation to the Philadelphia convention. But there were reports of other disturbances where farmers prevented courts from meeting or warned sheriffs to postpone auctions. Indeed, the malady that produced the Shays uprising had spread southward, as rumors from western Virginia now confirmed. "Good God! who besides a tory could have foreseen, or a Briton predicted them [the disorders]!" Washington lamented to Henry Knox.[5] Almost as Washington told Knox "that notwithstanding the boasted virtue of America, we are far gone in every

Rufus King. Engraving by T.
Kelly after an original painting
by Stuart.
Prints and Photographs Division

A Massachusetts delegate to
the Continental Congress in
New York, Rufus King was
gloomy about the prospects for
the success of the Philadelphia
convention.

thing ignoble and bad," he learned of his appointment to the Philadelphia convention. Washington tried to avoid the call of duty, but was convinced by Madison that his presence "could not be spared from the Deputation," chiefly because of "the advantage of having your name in the front of the appointment as a mark of the earnestness of Virginia" in constitutional reform.[6] Washington protested, but Madison prevailed. Once the leading citizens in the other twelve states heard Washington was bound for Philadelphia they needed little urging when called for service.

Meanwhile, Hamilton had his problems in New York. The entrenched state political machine dominated by George Clinton was enamored with the status quo. In the New York senate, a resolution supporting the forthcoming Philadelphia convention passed by a single vote.[7] Ultimately, when the New York delegation was chosen, Hamilton was added as a bow to the Manhattan merchants who also favored "energetic government"; but there was no other real advocate of reform on the list. Around Boston, where the disgusted merchants had more influence, a Bay State delegation took shape as solidly in favor of stringent reforms. And James Wilson's name on the Pennsylvania delegation promised the support of another tough-minded, experienced congressman whose thinking on the key matters of taxes and commercial regulation was broad-gauged. In nearly every case, the prospect of associating with Washington averted the chronic problem of nonattendance at the Philadelphia meeting.

Except for a few state politicians who loved their small ponds (George Clinton and Patrick Henry were notable "big fish"), most public men of stature in 1787 were ready to serve in order to act in Washington's company, and the remarkable outcome of the business was that only two significant Americans were not invited. Both were abroad. John Adams was serving as the American minister in London while Thomas Jefferson held a similar post in Paris. Considering all the tedium, horse-trading, and sensitive compromising that lay ahead, their absence was probably fortuitous. Since both tended to be political extremists, they might have been obstructionists to the moderation that eventually prevailed. An ocean away, Adams and Jefferson were left free to criticize the convention's handiwork with detached candor.

The only jarring note came from Rhode Island, where the state legislators were committed to paper money laws that made debt-ridden farmers the beneficiaries. By a twenty-two-vote majority the Rhode Island lawmakers rejected an invitation to

April 1787.

"Observations by J. M" (a copy taken by permission by Dan'l. Carroll sent to Ch.s Carroll of Carrolton)

Vices of the political system of the U. States

1. Failure of the States to comply with the constitutional requisitions.

1. This evil has been so fully experienced both during the war and since the peace, results so naturally from the number and independent authority of the States and has been so uniformly exemplified in every similar confederacy, that it may be considered as *not less* radically and permanently inherent in ~~the~~ than it is fatal to the object of the present System.

2. Encroachments by the States on the federal authority.

2. Examples of this are numerous and repetitions may be foreseen in almost every case where any favorite object of a State shall present a temptation. Among these examples are the wars and Treaties of Georgia with the Indians — The unlicensed compacts between Virginia and Maryland, and between Pen.a & N. Jersey — the troops raised and to be kept up by Mass.ts

send a delegation to Philadelphia. Their action made Madison fume. "Nothing can exceed the wickedness and folly which continue to reign there," Madison told Governor Randolph. "All sense of Character as well as of Right is obliterated. Paper money is still their idol, though it is debased to 8 to 1."[8]

Week by week news reports from other state capitals listing the appointed delegations drifted into New York, where the enfeebled Continental Congress met. Optimism was in short supply, nonetheless. Rufus King, serving in Congress and appointed a Massachusetts delegate, told a friend the situation on the eve of the Philadelphia convention was gloomy. "What the Convention may do at Philadelphia is very doubtful," King observed. "There are many well disposed men from the Southern States, who will attend the Convention; but the projects are so various, and all so short of the best, that my fears are by no means inferior to my Hopes on the subject." More enthusiastic was congressman William Grayson, who reported a rumor that Washington would be chosen to preside at the convention. "There are as great expectations here from the result of their deliberation."[9] Even the doubting Thomases realized what magnet was attracting fifty-five busy citizens from their other affairs. Washington's fame had accomplished a small miracle.

But gaining Washington's promise to attend the Philadelphia convention was only the first of Madison's preliminary preparations for the May gathering. With his scholarly turn of mind, Madison felt compelled to delve into the histories of other republics and confederations as he searched for examples of past failures and successes. The result was Madison's manuscript "Notes on Ancient and Modern Confederacies," a historical look at Greek, Roman, and European attempts to make confederation government work. Out of his research Madison formed a kind of dos-and-don'ts meant to provide a useful guide when the delegates convened in May. Along the way, Madison also reread the works of David Hume, Montesquieu, and other writers on modern constitutions. By the time Madison finished his scholarly explorations, he was back serving in the Continental Congress, where between daily meetings he found time for one last look at the impotent confederation. Working by candlelight in his rooming-house on Maiden Lane, Madison finished his "Vices of the Political System of the United States." As the first tulips appeared around New York's waterfront Battery, Madison boarded the Philadelphia stagecoach.

The point of Madison's reading and writing was to prepare himself for a leading role at the Philadelphia convention. In common with educated men of his generation, Madison believed libraries were intellectual workshops where books could be consulted to provide utilitarian knowledge. Hardly a knowledgeable American of Madison's day questioned the dictum preached by Hume that "the same causes lead to the same effects," so that Madison's research was of a practical bent. By learning where a Greek republic took false steps, by diagnosing the problems of the Helvetic Confederation, Madison hoped to learn ways of correcting the abuses inherent in the Articles of Confederation. Most important, by using these guideposts from the past, Madison expected to evolve a theory for American republicanism that would become a useful tool at the forthcoming Philadelphia convention. Madison's "bookishness" was great with purpose.

"We All Look Up to Virginia for Examples"

George Washington. Portrait attributed to Joseph Wright. *Courtesy of the Cleveland Museum of Art, Hinman B. Hurlbut Collection*

Washington said little at the Philadelphia convention, but his presence lent an aura of integrity to the proceedings. Many delegates assumed that Washington would become the first president, and this assumption may have affected their work in drafting the article on the presidency.

Monday, May 14, 1787, was the official date set for opening the Philadelphia convention; but only a handful of delegates had reached the City of Brotherly Love the preceding weekend and except for the Pennsylvanians no delegation was present. The Virginia delegates were among the first arrivals, and Washington's arrival on May 13 stirred the local citizens. Without a quorum, the convention was stymied and required to meet daily only to adjourn until enough delegations answered the roll call. Perhaps at Madison's suggestion, the Virginians decided to meet informally

each day to discuss a plan of action. Most of them stayed at the Indian Queen, a hostelry noted for good food and drink, where their talks probably were held as they awaited a full quorum. Once in Philadelphia, the delegates perceived an expectant mood in the city. "The Expectations & Hopes of all the Union center in this Convention," George Mason wrote his son. "God grant that we may be able to concert effectual Means of preserving our Country from the Evils which threaten us."[10]

For several hours each day the Virginia delegates discussed a plan which by tacit agreement was to form a blueprint for the convention. Not for a moment was a patchwork of amendments to the Articles of Confederation considered. After attending the Virginia caucus and sharing a cordial glass or two with other delegations, Mason noted an important drift in the conversations:

> The most prevalent Idea, in the principal States seems to be a total Alteration of the present fœderal System and substituting a great National Council, or Parliament, consisting of two Branches of the Legislature . . . with full legislative Powers upon all the Objects of the Union; and an Executive: and to make the several State Legislatures subordinate to the National. . . .

There in a nutshell was the Virginia Plan, which was ready by May 25, when twenty-nine delegates answered the roll call to make official business possible. Chiefly the work of Madison, the Virginia Plan was to provide the mechanism for debate and, after much revision and numerous amendments, it became the Constitution.

To understand why the Virginia delegation played such a dominant role on the eve of the convention, one must know something about the political geography of the United States in 1787, which differed radically from modern times. Virginia was then the largest and most populous state, with a leadership role in politics dating back to the Stamp Act crisis. Massachusetts was to New England a similar bellwether state, so that beyond the Connecticut River the tone and style of politics were Boston-dominated. The middle states of New York and Pennsylvania often exerted strong leadership, while New Jersey and Delaware occasionally identified with their neighbor's interests. Maryland was a slaveholding region of plantations inclined to go along with the southern viewpoint, but somewhat jealous of the leadership role exerted by Virginia. North Carolina tended to stay in step with Virginia, but South Carolina was unpredictable except on slavery, where her planters adamantly opposed any outside interference whatever. Georgia was sparsely settled, the "poor relation" of the South, but growing enough to feel hurt when her interests seemed ignored.

Blessed with wealth, manpower, and seasoned leaders, Virginia plainly stood out. Accordingly, her representatives at national political gatherings assumed responsible roles handily if not jealously. John Adams flattered the vanity of Patrick Henry in 1776 when he wrote on the eve of Independence: "Your intimation that the session of your representative body would be long, gave me great pleasure, because we all look up to Virginia for examples." Not much had changed in the intervening decade. Thus when the convention started tackling the problems which brought its delegates together, nothing was more natural than that the Virginia governor, Edmund Randolph, would lay the caucus plan before the whole body as the focus for discussions. On the first day, the only real business conducted was the unani-mous election of Washington as the presiding officer and the appointment of a rules

Edmund Randolph. Portrait by Flavius Fisher.
Courtesy of the Virginia State Library

As governor of the Old Dominion, Edmund Randolph served as head of the Virginia delegation in 1787.

committee. Nine more delegates arrived over the weekend so that on May 29 their work began in earnest. Throughout the ensuing weeks, some delegates went home to tend sick spouses and others to look after personal business; while some (like two New Yorkers) left because they thought the convention was going too far or was up to no good. Befuddled, penurious New Hampshire was not fully represented until July 23. Nonetheless, forty-two delegates persisted—despite frayed nerves, hot weather, pesky flies, illnesses, and even suspicions of what other delegates were up to—so that they would not disappoint their constituents or themselves.

Unquestionably, the delegates realized the eyes of the new nation were on them. Jefferson, when he read the list of delegates printed in a newspaper, told John Adams what appeared to be a common feeling about the fifty-five chosen to serve: "It is really an assembly of demigods."[11] Serving in Washington's presence, meeting for several hours each day and talking more at suppers later, the delegates became aware of their responsibilities. "For my own Part, I never before felt myself in such a Situation," George Mason confessed to his namesake, "and declare I wou'd not, upon pecuniary Motives, serve in this Convention for a thousand pounds per Day. The Revolt from Great Britain, & the Formations of our new Governments at that time, were nothing compared with the great Business now before us."[12] Upon the outcome of the convention, Mason added, depended "the Happiness or Misery of Millions yet unborn," so that a participant almost found "the Operations of the human Understanding" suspended.

From early June onward the delegates, committed to staying in Philadelphia come what may, worked unceasingly to deserve the nation's confidence. Washington's diary entries—"Attended in Convention," or "In Convention"—conceal the depths of a human drama enacted in the State House as conflicting interests were revealed in the debates over the Virginia Plan. To prevent public speculation and allow the freest range of debate on issues, the delegates decided to prohibit reporting of their sessions and any leak of information to even a wife or relative was forbidden. "I am sorry they began their deliberations by so abominable a precedent as that of tying up the tongues of their members," Jefferson observed.[14] But the truth was that the delegates wanted to speak freely and prevent a running criticism of key issues. No delegate explained their decision with more clarity than George Mason:

All Communications of the Proceedings are forbidden, during the Sitting of the Convention: this I think was a necessary precaution, to prevent misrepre-

Resolutions proposed by Mr. Randolph in Convention

May 29. 1787.

1. Resolved that the articles of Confederation ought to be so corrected & enlarged as to accomplish the objects proposed by their institution; namely. "common defence, security of liberty and general welfare."

2. Res⁴. therefore that the right of suffrage in the National Legislature ought to be proportioned to the Quotas of contribution, or to the number of free inhabitants, as the one or the other rule may seem best in different cases.

3. Res⁴. that the national Legislature ought to consist of two branches.

4. Res⁴. that the members of the first branch of the national Legislature ought to be elected by the people of the several States every   for the term of   ; to be of the age of   years at least, to receive a liberal stipends by which they may be compensated for the devotion of their time to public service; to be ineligible to any office established by a particular State, or under the authority of the United States, except those peculiarly belonging to the functions of the first branch, during the term of service, and for the space of   after its expiration; to be incapable of re-election for the space of   after the expiration of their term of service, and to be subject to recall.

5. Resol⁴. that the members of the second branch of the national Legislature ought to be elected by those of the first, out of a proper number of persons nominated by the individual Legislatures, to be of the age of   years at least,

to

James Madison's notes for May 29, "Resolutions proposed by Mr. Randolph in Convention." *Manuscript Division*

James Madison's decision to keep daily notes on the convention debates resulted in an invaluable record. Here Madison records the speech by Governor Edmund Randolph of Virginia that preceded his introduction of the Virginia Plan.

Edmund Randolph's copy of the Committee of Detail at work, July 26, 1787. *Manuscript Division*

The Virginia delegation arrived at Philadelphia on time and, finding others tardy, caucused to devise a scheme for a republican government with a two-house legislature, an executive branch, and a national court of justice. Introduced by Governor Randolph, the plan served as a framework for what would become the Constitution.

sentation, or mistakes; there being a material Difference between the appearance of a Subject in it's first crude, indigested Shape, and after it shall have been properly matured & arranged.[15]

Years later, Madison suggested that public disclosure of the debates would have locked a speaker into an argument and made it difficult for him to change his mind. In 1830 Madison told a historian what seems to have been a common judgment in 1787—"no constitution would ever have been adopted by the convention if the debates had been public."[16]

The convention thus began with remarkable unanimity on how to proceed. The willingness to debate the Virginia Plan and the May 30 vote to establish "a national governt . . . consisting of a supreme Legislative Executive & Judiciary" was recognition that the Articles of Confederation were finished. The delegates realized they had the summer months for their work, and they were aware that the confederation was dying of natural causes. With the Virginia Plan before them, the delegates

James Wilson. Painting by James Peale.
Photograph in the Prints and Photographs Division
Pennsylvania lawyer James Wilson was an influential proponent at the convention for a strong national government.

moved over some of the major hurdles (supremacy of national laws over state measures, including taxes and commercial regulation). The early tone set was for hard work, starting after breakfast and continuing until late in the afternoon. Usually five hours were consumed in the talks, and sometimes they argued points past the four o'clock dining hour. Monday through Saturday they watched Washington turn the chair over to Nathaniel Gorham each morning (as chairman of the special committee "of the Whole House on the State of the Union"). Then the business of the day was tackled with dispatch, frankness, and sometimes petulance. Nobody pretended this was a love feast, for their main business was the saving of the republic.

The pattern of debate and the general outlines of the new government were established by June 13. Using the Virginia Plan, the delegates had accepted the general outlines and only balked on the matters of electing a president and permitting Congress to veto "all [state] Laws which they shd. judge to be improper," and the composition of the senate.[17] Generally the delegates agreed that there should be a single person acting as the executive, that the lower house of the legislature should be chosen by "some equitable ratio of representation," and that there should be a supreme tribunal for the judicial branch. They also agreed that new states could be admitted to the original union with "a republican Constitution," that amendments to the new plan of government ought to be possible, and that their final draft of a constitution ought to be sent to special conventions in each state for final ratification.

The accomplishments made by June 13 were impressive, but the discussion of several controversial propositions had been temporarily postponed. Foremost was the matter of proportional representation, which the Virginia Plan favored for both houses of Congress. The small-state delegations never liked this idea, and before the month was out they made no attempt to conceal their distress. Northern delegates were uneasy with the carryover proposition from confederation days providing for the counting of three-fifths of all slaves in the assignment of congressional seats. Second thoughts about the right of Congress to nullify any state law surfaced, despite Madison's insistence that this was a paramount issue affording a vital means of checking demagogues.

Madison was on his feet often, but not as much as James Wilson. The Pennsylvania lawyer, whom a fellow-delegate characterized as "the foremost in legal and *pg 98.*

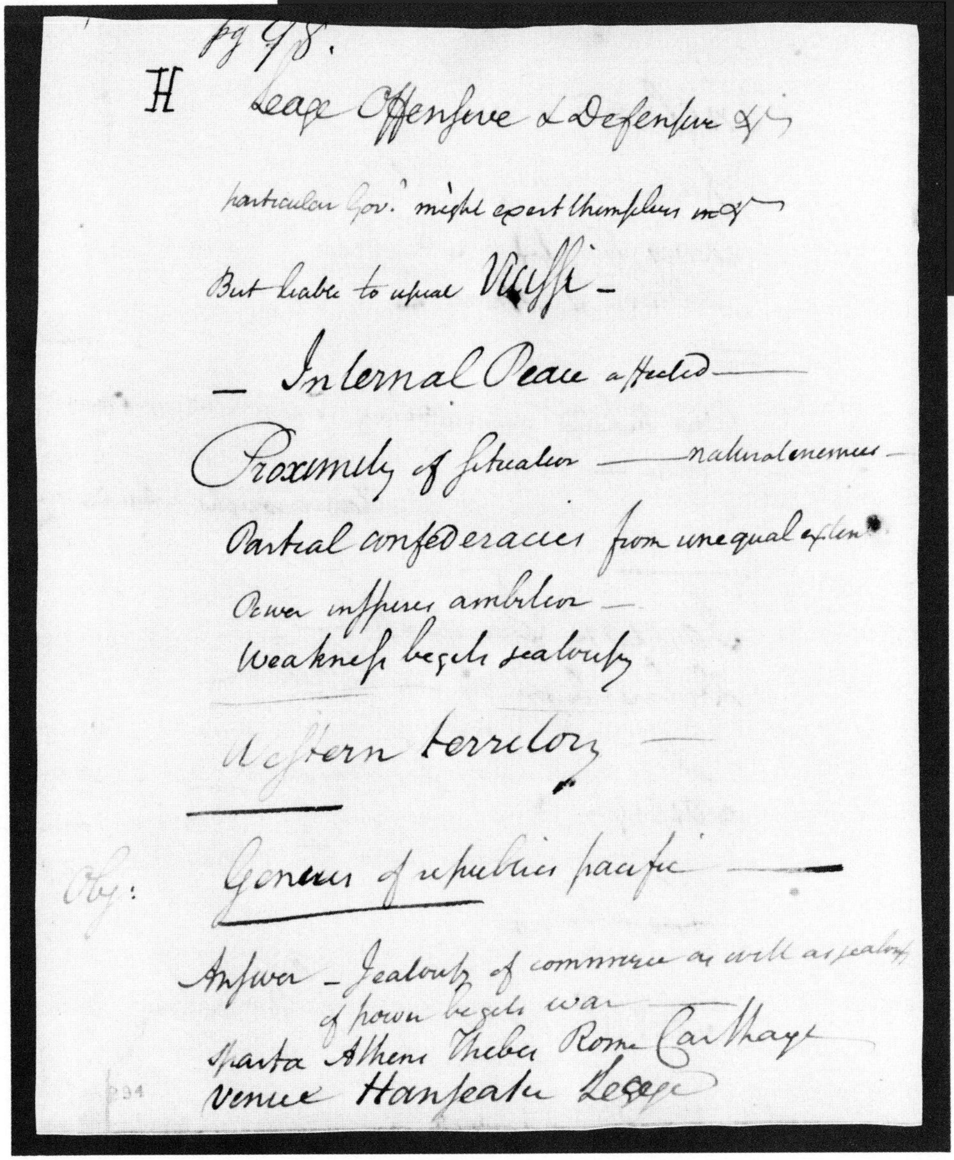

H League Offensive & Defensive &c

particular Gov.ᵗ might exert themselves &c

But liable to usual Vicissi –

— Internal Peace affected —

Proximity of Situation —— natural enemies —

Partial confederacies from unequal extent

Power inspires ambition —

Weakness begets jealousy

Western territory —

Obj: Genius of republics pacific —— —

Answer – Jealousy of commerce as well as jealousy
of power begets war
Sparta Athens Thebes Rome Carthage
Venice Hanseatic League

Alexander Hamilton's notes for
his speech of June 18, 1787.
Manuscript Division

Hamilton favored a constitutional monarchy patterned
after the English system, but
he realized Americans would
not accept a king and admitted
this in his convention speeches.

political knowledge," was self-assured and confident.[18] On matters of law, the convention deferred to Wilson, who made no pretense of hiding his strong leanings toward an "energetic" national government. Alexander Hamilton was more disposed to increasing the powers of the national government than either Wilson or Madison, but after a speech which took up most of the June 18 session the New York delegate bolted for home, not to return until August.

Alexander Hamilton. Portrait by John Trumbull.
Photograph in the Prints and Photographs Division

Hamilton was married to a New York heiress and had the support of the New York mercantile community when he went to Philadelphia to plead for a stronger central government.

In firing what seemed like a parting shot, Hamilton confessed his admiration of the British constitution and monarchy, adding "that he doubted much whether any thing short of it would do in America."[19] Hamilton, shielded by the secrecy rule, revealed that he was ready to go further than any man present and swallow up the states "by substituting a general Govt." But Hamilton admitted public opinion stood in the way of his solution to their problems, so he proposed an alternative to the Virginia Plan that created a senate with members serving for life ("during good behavior"), a president that was a king in everything but name, and a supreme court appointed for life. Few of the delegates took Hamilton seriously, although many of them acknowledged that frequent elections contributed to their current problems.

Madison, another outspoken nationalist in the convention, was more politic and persistent than either Hamilton or Wilson. During the daily meetings (and he never missed a session) Madison tried to save all the leading features of the Virginia Plan. At night he took his shorthand notes to a Walnut Street boardinghouse and captured in writing the speeches delivered a few hours earlier. His research and experience paid off in that whenever Madison spoke the delegates strained to hear. "What is very remarkable," a Georgia delegate noted, was that "every Person seems to acknowledge his greatness. He blends together the profound politician, with the Scholar . . . tho' he cannot be called an Orator, he is a most agreable, eloquent, and convincing Speaker."[20] Madison believed that proportional representation was a key issue, along with the possibility for vetoing obnoxious state laws. He forced these ideas into the Virginia Plan, and when they were both jeopardized by compromises, Madison began to lose faith in the outcome of the convention.

Yet the spirit of the meeting was one of give-and-take, and since strong nationalists like Madison and Wilson were unwilling to compromise on certain issues, it fell to less prominent men to keep the convention together. The small-state delegations insisted that votes in a congress based on population alone would destroy their power; Madison and the other nationalists argued that only by this scheme could republicanism survive. Early on, John Dickinson from Delaware suggested a two-house system, with the lower chamber based on population and the upper one on equal votes for all states. The arguments raged until Benjamin Franklin pleaded with the delegates to stop "groping as it were in the dark to find political truth" and turn to prayer.[22] After some embarrassing moments, Dr. Franklin's proposition was

John Dickinson. Etching by Albert Rosenthal after a painting by Charles Willson Peale. *Prints and Photographs Division*

Noted as a powerful writer of pamphlets in the 1770s, John Dickinson helped draft the Articles of Confederation. He was a fair-minded moderate who played an important role when disputes marred the proceedings in Philadelphia.

Roger Sherman. Engraving by S. S. Jocelyn from a painting by Earle. *Prints and Photographs Division*

When the small- and large-state delegations could not reach agreement on representation, Roger Sherman of Connecticut proposed a moderate plan that allowed proportional representation in the lower house and an equal vote for all states in the upper chamber. Sherman's "Connecticut Compromise" drew the convention back from the brink of failure.

dropped. The session adjourned with the New Jersey and Virginia delegates convinced of each other's unbridled selfishness.

Connecticut delegate Oliver Ellsworth stepped into the breach created by the pigheadedness of the likes of Wilson and Paterson. Wilson was arrogant, while Paterson (from Wilson's neighbor-state of New Jersey) was belligerent. Wilson tried to sidetrack Ellsworth's plea for a Senate where each state held equal representation. Ellsworth, aware that some give and take was necessary, spoke plainly. "He trusted that on this middle ground a compromise would take place," Madison recorded. "He did not see that it could on any other."

There were objections and the pace of debate quickened without producing visible signs of progress. "We are now at a full stop," Roger Sherman told the delegates, "and nobody he supposed meant that we shd. break up without doing something."[23] Sherman suggested a committee might save them from further treadmilling, and before the day ended twelve men were picked to find a way out of the convention's dilemma.

When the committee reported, it offered a face-saving gesture to the large states by giving the lower house the exclusive power to originate "money bills," and thus the first shot at control of the nation's purse strings. Not much solace there for Wilson or Madison, but it was the spirit of the proposal that counted. On July 14

William Paterson. Portrait by Henry Harrison after James Sharples.
Courtesy of the New Jersey State Museum

William Paterson fought for the New Jersey Plan to the point that some delegates feared the Philadelphia convention would fail in its mission.

the large-state delegates made their final bid for victory when they asked for an apportioned senate that would have meant, for example, one vote for Rhode Island and five for Virginia. Nothing doing, the small state delegates said. Luther Martin of Maryland would not be bullied. "The States that please to call themselves large, are the weakest in the Union," he insisted. "Look at Massts. Look at Virga. Are they efficient States? He was for letting a separation take place if they desired it," Madison recorded.

1.

1. Resolved, That a union of the States merely federal ought to be the sole object of the exercise of the powers vested in this Convention.

2. Resolved, That the Articles of the Confederation ought to be so revised, corrected, and enlarged as to render the federal Constitution adequate to the exigencies of Government, and the preservation of the Union—

3. Resolved, That the federal Government of the United States ought to consist of a supreme Legislative, Executive, and Judiciary—

4. Resolved, That the powers of Legislation ought to be vested in Congress.

5. Resolved, That in Addition to the powers vested in the united States in Congress by the present existing Articles of Confederation, they be authorised to pass Acts for levying a Duty or Duties on all Goods and Merchandize of foreign Growth or Manufacture imported into any

84

William Paterson's New Jersey Plan.
Manuscript Division
The New Jersey delegates surrendered their "one-state, one-vote" privileges from earlier times reluctantly. Delegate William Paterson, who later served on the Supreme Court, wanted to block the Virginia Plan for proportional representation by ensuring small states equal voices in national deliberations.

John Lansing's copy of Robert Yates's notes on the debates for July 5, 1787.
Manuscript Division

Early in July the deadlock between small and large state delegations was broken, a fact recorded by New York delegate Robert Yates shortly before he left Philadelphia in disappointment.

Perhaps the delegates had been working too hard, for they had kept moving, with no interruptions except for the sabbath and only a two-day respite for the hallowed Fourth of July, as they sought an escape from their impass. (Washington added a bit of variety to his life by sitting for portrait-painter Charles Willson Peale in the early hours "before the meeting of the Convention.") At last, on July 16 a committee report recommending the senate-equality compromise barely passed, five votes to four, with Massachusetts divided. Stubbornness within the Bay State delegation opened a crack just wide enough for the compromise to slip through.

With our hindsight we see how the whole constitution began falling into shape after that critical vote, but at the time the hotheads made the situation appear extremely dangerous. Governor Randolph ranted and raved, and suggested that they adjourn the convention so "that the large States might consider the steps proper to be taken in the present solemn crisis of the business." Small-stater Paterson, not to be outdone, agreed "that it was high time for the Convention to adjourn, that the rule of secrecy ought to be rescinded, and that our Constituents should be consulted."[22] If Randolph was serious about making a motion to adjourn and go home, Paterson threatened, "he would second it with all his heart."

Had these rash suggestions been followed, the end result can only be imagined. Wilson and Madison were angry and disappointed, too, but the vote stuck and—to everybody's ultimate great relief—the convention never was in jeopardy again. The following nine working days of the convention were conducted in a new atmosphere of solid accomplishment as the powers of Congress and federal court jurisdictions were defined. Madison still wanted a means of controlling irresponsible state legislatures, and the more he thought about local demagogues the more he pleaded for such a check. A better way to handle the problem, some delegates thought, was through a supreme-law-of-the-land clause. Still smarting from the bruises of July 16, Madison at the moment thought otherwise. The main question had been decided, however. A constitution of some kind would be ready before the fall harvests.

A Great Compromise and a Great Lesson

The Convention in session. Engraving from Charles A. Goodrich, *A History of the United States of America*, 1823. *Rare Book and Special Collections Division*

This idyllic depiction fails to represent the actual convention and debates, but when it appeared in 1823 Americans approved the idea of unity that pervades the work.

One valuable lesson that emerged from the July 16 vote was the beginning of an American political tradition that mixed sportsmanship with common sense. This tradition would last until the eve of the Civil War, so its emergence at the Philadelphia convention was in a sense almost as important as the constitution itself. Tied to the republican idea that the majority must rule in a self-governing society, the tradition was typified in Madison's reaction to the July 16 compromise. Two days after that disappointing vote, Madison wrote Jefferson without a hint of his chagrin.

> I am still under the mortification of being restrained from disclosing a part of their proceedings. As soon as I am at liberty I will endeavor to make amends for my silence. . . . I have taken lengthy notes of every thing that has yet passed, and mean to go on with the drudgery, if no indisposition obliges me to discontinue it.

Madison added that "the public mind is very impatient for the event, and various reports are circulating which tend to inflame the curiosity."[24]

So far as Madison could tell, the average American accepted the injunction of secrecy in good grace. "I do not learn . . . that any discontent is expressed at the concealment; and have little doubt that the people will be as ready to receive as we shall be able to propose, a Government that will secure their liberties & happiness."[23] Madison's summation of the public mood is not that of an angry loser, but of a good sport who concedes that his judgment is not always infallible.

Historians have written about the July 16 vote as the "Great Compromise," but can scarcely overstress the enormous importance of that event in American history. James Wilson, Madison, and the other outspoken advocates of predominant national government did not stalk out of the convention in a huff, as the extremists of 1860 would do; instead, the losers on July 16 furnished an example for all the world to follow. The lesson worth remembering was: Believe in your position and work for its success, but learn to live with a political compromise that provides something less than complete victory. In that spirit of accommodation, the republic was saved in 1787; and a long, bloody war could have been avoided if the same counsels had prevailed seventy-three years later.

Once the problem of a national-state government relationship was solved, the convention moved with uncommon speed. More time was spent debating the presidential term and the means of electing the chief executive than on what he was supposed to do, once in office. The president would be commander-in-chief of the armed forces (to keep a civilian in charge), and he would have a cabinet shaped along British constitutional lines. He could pardon offenses against the United States ("except in Cases of Impeachment"), and he would carry on foreign relations, including the making of treaties, with the advice and consent of the Senate. He was not to be a monarch, for the presidential term was limited, and the Senate was to

provide a nominal check on his several powers. Unlike the restrictions and allow-ances specified for Congress, there was no clause listing presidential dos-and-don'ts. The delegates wavered between leaving the choice of president up to Congress or involving the states directly, but finally voted for an electoral college with the members selected by the state legislatures. For a time they considered a single seven-year term, and discussed at length the means of removing an unfit president. With their sense of history, the delegates alluded to Charles I and Charles II of England as examples of monarchs who abused their power, and finally decided that the chief executive ought to be impeachable for "high crimes and misdemeanors." Exactly what the president's duties and powers would be was a secondary concern, since Congress was expected to be the strongest branch of government.

After some minor wrangling, the convention moved toward its first adjourn-ment. A committee of detail was selected to take all the resolutions and decisions made thus far and incorporate them into a working draft of a constitution. Before that took place, however, such details as the procedures for admitting new states brought out the worst and best in several delegates. Elbridge Gerry of Massachu-setts was afraid that if new states were admitted without limit they would in time outnumber their eastern partners to "oppress commerce, and drain our wealth into the Western Country." Gerry moved for a provision that new states "shall never exceed in number . . . such of the States as shall accede to this confederation." Another New Englander, Roger Sherman, took a broader view. "We are providing for our posterity, for our children & our grand Children," Sherman reminded the convention, "who would be as likely to be citizens of the new Western States, as of the old States."[25] Discrimination against the new states was appealing to both the Connecticut and Massachusetts delegations as a whole, however, and the measure (that would have kept the seaboard states in control of Congress) lost by a single vote.

Much of the Virginia Plan remained intact as the convention prepared to turn its work over to the committee, but Madison's favorite provision of a veto on state legislation failed to win support. The smaller states were dead-set against what seemed a threat to their power, and within the Virginia delegation Governor Randolph and George Mason both opposed the proposition. Grudgingly, Madison backed down but indicated the issue was not yet settled despite the three-ayes-to-seven-nays vote, which seemed to kill the measure.[26] Most delegates thought that a

WE the People of the States of New-Hampfhire, Maffachufetts, Rhode-Ifland and Providence Plantations, Connecticut, New-York, New-Jerfey, Pennfylvania, Delaware, Maryland, Virginia, North-Carolina, South-Carolina, and Georgia, do ordain, declare and eftablifh the following Conftitution for the Government of Ourfelves and our Pofterity.

ARTICLE I.

The ftile of this Government fhall be, " The United States of America."

II.

The Government fhall confift of fupreme legiflative, executive and judicial powers.

III.

The legiflative power fhall be vefted in a Congrefs, to confift of two feparate and diftinct bodies of men, a Houfe of Reprefentatives, and a Senate; ~~each of which fhall in all cafes have a negative on the other.~~ The Legiflature fhall meet on the firft Monday in December ~~in every year.~~ *unlefs a different day fhall be appointed by law—*

IV.

Sect. 1. The Members of the Houfe of Reprefentatives fhall be chofen every fecond year, by the people of the feveral States comprehended within this Union. The qualifications of the electors fhall be the fame, from time to time, as thofe of the electors in the feveral States, of the moft numerous branch of their own legiflatures.

Sect. 2. Every Member of the Houfe of Reprefentatives fhall be of the age of twenty-five years at leaft; fhall have been a citizen ~~in~~ the United States for at leaft ~~three~~ years before his election; and fhall be, at the time of his election, ~~a refident~~ of the State in which he fhall be chofen.

Sect. 3. The Houfe of Reprefentatives fhall, at its firft formation, and until the number of citizens and inhabitants fhall be taken in the manner herein after defcribed, confift of fixty-five Members, of whom three fhall be chofen in New-Hampfhire, eight in Maffachufetts, one in Rhode-Ifland and Providence Plantations, five in Connecticut, fix in New-York, four in New-Jerfey, eight in Pennfylvania, one in Delaware, fix in Maryland, ten in Virginia, five in North-Carolina, five in South-Carolina, and three in Georgia.

Sect. 4. As the proportions of numbers in the different States will alter from time to time; as fome of the States may hereafter be divided; as others may be enlarged by addition of territory; as two or more States may be united; as new States will be erected within the limits of the United States, the Legiflature fhall, in each of thefe cafes, regulate the number of reprefentatives by the number of inhabitants, according to the ~~provifions herein after made~~, at the rate of one for every forty thoufand. *provided every ftate fhall have one reprefentative*

Sect. 5. All bills for raifing or appropriating money, and for fixing the falaries of the officers of government, fhall originate in the Houfe of Reprefentatives, and fhall not be altered or amended by the Senate. No money fhall be drawn from the public Treafury, but in purfuance of appropriations that fhall originate in the Houfe of Reprefentatives.

Sect. 6. The Houfe of Reprefentatives fhall have the fole power of impeachment. It fhall choofe its Speaker and other officers.

Sect. 7. Vacancies in the Houfe of Reprefentatives fhall be fupplied by writs of election from the executive authority of the State, in the reprefentation from which they fhall happen.

V.

Committee of Detail report, printed by Claypoole and Dunlap.
Manuscript Division

Finished drafts of the committee reports were printed and passed out to delegates to help them deliberate more carefully. Great secrecy was enjoined from printers Claypoole and Dunlap, who kept their trust and did not print the final draft until after the September 17 signing ceremony.

Left Baltimore 2 August.

August 4th

Returned to Philada. The committee of Convention ready to report. Their report in the hands of Dunlop the printer to strike off copies for the members.

Augt. 6. Convention met. present 8 states. report delivered in by Mr. Rutledge. — read — Convention adjourned till to-morrow to give the ~~members~~ members an opportunity to consider the report.

Proposed to Mr. D. Carrol. Mr. Jenifer — Mr Mercer & Mr. Martin to meet to confer on the report, and to prepare ourselves to act in unison. —

Met at Mr. Carrolls lodgings in the afternoon. I repeated the object of our meeting, and proposed that we should take the report up by paragraphs and give our opinions thereon.

Mr. Mercer wished to know of me whether I thought Maryland would embrace such a system, ~~and~~ I told him I did not know, but I presumed the people would not object to a wise system. He extended this idea to the other gentlemen, ~~with~~

clause in the committee resolution establishing acts of congress and treaties as "the supreme Law" was enough. Madison considered the gesture a poor consolation prize.[27]

A much-needed adjournment on July 26 allowed the special committee ten days to sift through all the adopted resolutions, arrange them in working order, and produce a report for further corrections or additions. Significantly, Governor Randolph was named to the committee rather than Madison, making James Wilson the strongest personality on the five-man board. The others (Rutledge, Gorham, and Ellsworth) were more moderate than the delegates who had talked the most, which might explain their selection.

In the meantime, news came from the Continental Congress, meeting in New York. Although shorthanded because so many delegates were working in Philadelphia, the Congress passed its last important bill when a report on the Northwest Territory was written into law. For three years they had talked about a way of organizing the territory above the Ohio River, and at long last a bill (scarcely recognizable as the one Jefferson wrote in 1784) became law.

What the Northwest Ordinance accomplished was the creation of a system for easing unsettled territory into the Union in stages of population growth, while extending to the settlers what amounted to a bill of rights. This was no mean achievement. The law also established a workable survey plan for settlements on the frontier. Almost as an afterthought, the bill also dealt with the matter of slavery (an issue that some delegates at Philadelphia wished to avoid) by providing that "neither slavery nor involuntary servitude [shall exist] in the said territory." Passage of the ordinance gave the struggling confederation some hope that public land sales would stave off public creditors, which it did. Far more important, however, was the precedent set for national growth that would prevail until the Pacific was reached. At the moment, its chief virtue was that the ordinance proved Congress was capable of enacting legislation of permanent worth. However, so much attention was already focused on Philadelphia that the ordinance created little stir, except with a few congressmen who were convinced the anticipated western land sales would create a "great fund for the extinguishment of the National debt."[28]

Week after week slavery was ignored by the delegates wary of mentioning the incendiary issue. At last Madison touched on the subject when he said in blunt terms on June 30 that not a state's size but its position on slavery was the major dividing line in the Union. Gouverneur Morris pricked southern consciences when he asked whether the three-fifths compromise was fair. If slaves were counted because they constituted wealth, Morris asked, why not include other forms of wealth in proportioning the legislative strength of a state? Charles Cotesworth Pinckney, alarmed by this suggestion, argued that South Carolina "has in one year exported to the amount of £600,000 Sterling all [of] which was the fruit of the labor of her blacks. Will she be represented in proportion to this amount? She will not."[29] When the committee of detail was formed, Pinckney reminded them "that if the Committee should fail to insert some security to the Southern States agst. an emancipation of slaves, and taxes on exports," the South Carolina delegation would vote against their report. That threat stopped any movement to insert a temporizing statement on slavery.[30]

One result of the debate over slavery was that another compromise had to be worked out, and by August 25 the outlines of a horse-trade appeared. The northern delegates voted for the three-fifths compromise and with southern help they forestalled the prohibition of an American navigation law (that would have prevented shipping Yankee cargoes in foreign ships); in return, the Southerners retained the ban in taxing exports, and Congress was forbidden to interfere with "the migration or importation of such persons as the several states shall think proper to admit" until 1808.[31] Of all the compromises in the final draft, this one was potentially the most dangerous. The delegates thus avoided using the word *slaves* but the price-tag was, in time, drenched in blood.

A compromise with the free-state delegates over the slave trade was reached by the Southerners, General Pinckney reminded the convention, when he praised Northerners for their understanding of the southern position. When the northern shipping losses during the Revolution were considered, Pinckney said, along with the northern delegates' "liberal conduct towards the views of South Carolina . . . he thought it proper that no fetters should be imposed on the power of making commercial regulations." In his notes, Madison made an asterisk to explain "the liberal conduct." Pinckney "meant the permission to import slaves. An understanding on the two subjects of *navigation* and *slavery,* had taken place between those parts of the Union."

James Madison's notes for August 8, 1787, including Gouverneur Morris's remarks on slavery.
Manuscript Division

Gouverneur Morris of Pennsylvania was plain-spoken when the convention debated representation. He wanted no allowance made for slaves and called slavery "the curse of heaven on the States where it prevailed." Despite Morris's protests, the so-called "three-fifths compromise" was adopted, giving the southern states some recognition of their slave holdings.

Another bargain had been struck, but the only loud dissenter was one of the largest slaveholders in the convention—George Mason. When a northern delegate (although admitting his personal distaste for the business) urged the speedy dispatch of the slave-trade clause, Mason thought the time for truth had arrived. He blamed the "infernal traffic" on "the avarice of British Merchants," as he recounted the history of slave importations during colonial days, and observed that since the Revolution both Maryland and Virginia had stopped slave importations.

All this would be in vain if S. Carolina & Georgia be at liberty to import. The Western people are already calling out for slaves . . . and will fill that Country with slaves if they can be got thro' S. Carolina & Georgia. Slavery discourages arts & manufactures. The poor despise labor when performed by slaves. . . . They produce the most pernicious effect on manners. Every master of slaves is born a petty tyrant. They bring the judgment of heaven on a Country.

Prophetically, Mason warned that unless they prohibited the slave trade, providence would intervene to punish "national sins" with "national calamities." He begged the delegates to grant the new government they were creating a "power to prevent the increase of slavery."[32]

Mason could have saved his breath, for the delegates on both sides of the sectional fence thought a bargain was a bargain. Ellsworth had the temerity to say that if slavery was as bad as Mason indicated, the convention should go the whole way and free all the slaves. Then he suggested that the final outcome was likely to be based on economics: "Let us not intermeddle." For as he and probably most of the delegates believed, "As population increases; poor laborers will be so plenty as to render slaves useless. Slavery in time will not be a speck in our Country."[33] Madison did not record the nodding of heads or the mumbling of "Hear! Hear!" But that must have been the reaction, for the slavery issue was settled then and there. As a constitutional issue, it would lie dormant until 1819.

By the last week in August, with the slavery problem apparently solved (a tax "not to exceed ten dollars" on each imported slave was a final concession), most delegates conceded they were nearing the end of their labors, although some became impatient and a few went home. Influential John Rutledge complained about "the tediousness of the proceedings" in mid-August and suggested the daily sessions be lengthened to speed up their business. The debates were extended to 4:00 P.M. for a time, but within a week the cutoff time was returned to 3:00 P.M The great

Luther Martin.
Courtesy Independence National Historical Park Collection

Large of body and loud of voice, Luther Martin of Maryland was a highly visible delegate. "He never speaks without tiring the patience of all who hear him," a fellow delegate wrote.

battles had been fought, so that much of the haggling now was over details. Among the defectors were outspoken Luther Martin and his cohort, John Francis Mercer. Madison, who had known Mercer for years, made a notation on the former Virginian's parting remark. "Mr. Mercer expressed his dislike of the whole plan, and [gave] his opinion that it never could succeed."[33] With such obstreperous men out of the way, however, the convention proceeded with more dispatch.

Late in August, the important matter of the public debt created to finance the Revolution came up when a special committee recommended that Congress "shall have power to fulfil the engagements which have been entered into" by the old Continental Congress. Everybody knew what was at issue, for although the old Continental currency was worthless, the war bonds issued after 1776 were still trading far below par value simply as speculative securities. When the convention first met, these "loan certificates" could be purchased for about thirty cents on the dollar, and Mason suggested that this promise of eventual redemption would touch off "speculations and [an] increase" of the pestilent practice of stock-jobbing. Mason wanted a distinction made "between the original creditors & those who purchased [securities] fraudulently of the ignorant and distressed." Gerry admitted frauds had occurred but objected to Mason's attack on speculators. "They keep up the value of the paper," Gerry insisted. "Without them there would be no market."

Randolph stepped into the fray, moving for an ambiguous change of wording. All debts contracted by the Continental Congress "shall be as valid agst the U. States under this constitution as under the Confederation."[34] This meant nothing or everything, depending on whether one's sympathies lay with those soldiers who had sold their paper promises for a few shillings or with the buyers who risked a repudiation. Only the Pennsylvania delegation voted against the change, and once the key clause passed no sharp rise in public certificates occurred. In other words, the delegates did not use their knowledge of what transpired in the convention for personal gain. The market in public securities remained sluggish for months, and no evidence has ever been cited to prove that a single delegate profited immediately from his vote on this issue.*

By late August the big compromises had been made, the sectional interests adjusted, and the small-state coteries mollified. Now the general outlines of the final draft were becoming clearer. The taxing power, and the right to borrow money and appropriate it, was meant to give Congress a dominant position in the new government. Much time had been spent setting the limits on congressional power, which seemed to be the delegates' chief concern at times; and more hours were allotted to discussing the way of electing a president than what he would do once in office. The court system was left in the barest outline form, with the presumption that the newly created Congress would fill in the details of numbers, jurisdictions, and other matters not specified in the section spelling out cases "arising under this Constitution."

Another special committee also recommended that the location of the national capital should be settled by Congress. An unspecified locale would be surveyed

---

*Charles A. Beard's work *An Economic Interpretation of the Constitution of the United States* (New York: Macmillan, 1913) was considered an exposé of the delegates cupidity when it first appeared. In fact, Beard used the extant treasury records to show that one delegate, William Livingston of New Jersey, held perhaps $100,000 in public securities in 1791, and a few New England delegates owned $20,000 or less. Whether they bought this paper in 1787 or later is not known. More to the point, the makers-and-shapers such as Hamilton and Madison apparently bought no securities whatever; and the biggest plunger of them all, Robert Morris, died a virtual bankrupt.

over ten square miles and become, in effect, a federal district under the jurisdiction of Congress. Between the lines, the exact site was still a matter of speculation, but the general agreement seemed to favor a mid-Atlantic region somewhere south of Philadelphia but north of Richmond. (At least four states were soon jockeying for position, since the plan revolved around gifts of land from "particular States, and the Acceptance of Congress.") The delegates also agreed to a kind of catch-all clause that granted Congress the power "to make all laws necessary and proper for carrying into execution the foregoing powers."[35] Madison tried to refine the language, but without success, and nobody appears to have thought the expression was anything like the carte blanche it became in the next century.

A few delegates were already worrying about the kinds of laws designed for local enhancement that latter-day cynics would call "pork-barrel" legislation. James McHenry of Maryland was concerned about funding for navigational aids in the Chesapeake Bay and thought a specific authorizing clause might be needed. Not to worry, he was told by Gouverneur Morris, for such matters would fall under the power of Congress "to provide for the common defence and general welfare."[36] It is helpful to remember that thirty-four of the fifty-five delegates were lawyers!

Before a final committee was chosen to polish the various sections with some rhetorical grace, several delegates voiced their anxieties. The electoral college for selecting the president had been approved, but in the event that no candidate had a majority, the Senate was to make a choice from the five leading candidates. Wilson said that the more he studied the office of president and combined it "with other parts of the plan, he was obliged to consider the whole as having a dangerous tendency to aristocracy; as throwing a dangerous power into the hands of the Senate."[37] Hamilton, back from his New York digression, joined in the attack. As reported by the committee, the president served for one seven-year term. "In this the President was a Monster elected for seven years," Hamilton said, and "he would be tempted to make use of corrupt influence to be continued in office." In short order the delegates voted to cut the presidential term to four years, make him reelectable, and changed the place of deciding close votes from the Senate to the House of Representatives, "the members from each State having one vote."[37]

This was progress made, all things considered, with breathtaking speed. For as the September 6 session ended, the delegates must have realized that the substantial work had been done. Two days later, they turned everything over to a committee of

Gouverneur Morris. Engraving
by Johnson, Fry & Co.
Prints and Photographs Division

Crippled by a stagecoach acci-
dent, Gouverneur Morris used
a wooden leg to move about the
State House. He was noted for
his brilliant, frank remarks
about the emerging
Constitution.

style charged with bringing in a final draft along with a covering letter to the old
congress in New York. The delegates made Samuel Johnson chairman of this
committee, adding Rufus King, Gouverneur Morris, Alexander Hamilton, and James
Madison as members. Then they adjourned for the weekend.

While Morris took over the business of turning all the resolutions into a readable
and relatively succinct constitution, the convention offered a few last-minute changes.
The amending process was enlarged by Madison, who suggested that both Congress and the state legislatures ought to be involved, and that an amendment would
become binding when ratified by three-fourths of the states. The alteration was
readily accepted. Perhaps worried that their proceedings had been high-handed and
legally doubtful, the delegates also decided to involve the Continental Congress.
Legally, the only way to proceed was for the Continental Congress to send the draft

constitution forward to the state legislatures for ratification or rejection; and most delegates believed that instead of thirteen, approval by nine states would be sufficient.[38] Thus the quasi-legal finally became the formally acceptable.

Or almost—for nothing of such magnitude could conclude harmoniously. A potential wrench-in-the-works was thrown by the head of the Virginia delegation, Edmund Randolph, who began to show the strain of his long sojourn in Philadelphia. Governor Randolph recalled that he had presented the Virginia Plan and admitted he favored "radical changes in the system of the Union." But the turn things took now worried him immensely, to the degree that unless the proposed constitution went to the states where ratifiying conventions "sh[oul]d be at liberty to offer amendments to the plan—and these submitted to a second General Convention" he would have to reserve judgment on the entire final report. Gerry came right behind Randolph, "urging the indecency and pernicious tendency of dissolving in so slight a manner, the solemn obligations of the articles of confederation."[39] We can almost see Madison's brows raised in disbelief. Had they been battling and bartering for three months to come to this—was another general convention in the works?

Hamilton moved swiftly to ward off the second-convention threat by recommending that the proposed plan of government be sent to the Continental Congress for transmission to the states, where special conventions would vote and if they approved "the said Constitution, such approbation shall be binding and conclusive upon the State . . . [and] shall take effect between the States assenting thereto." This quieted Gerry's fears that Congress might be bypassed, but the other delegates were not pleased. What finally came forth was a simple statement that ratification by nine states was "sufficient for the Establishment of this Constitution between the States so ratifying the Same." If Rhode Island or any other recalcitrant state wanted to stay out of the Union, that was an alternative the delegates were prepared to accept.

When the delegates assembled on September 12, Gouverneur Morris had finished his report and the covering letter to the Continental Congress. As Madison said later, credit for "the finish given to the style and arrangement . . . fairly belongs to the pen of Mr. Morris," the chore being assigned to him by Chairman Johnson "with the ready concurrence of the others. A better choice could not have been made, as the performance of the task proved."[40] Madison recalled that few changes

No state shall, without the consent of Congress, lay imposts or duties on imports or exports, but to the use of the treasury of the United States; keep troops nor ships of war in time of peace, nor enter into any agreement or compact with another state, nor with any foreign power. nor engage in war, unless it shall be actually invaded, or the danger of delay.

II.

Sect. 1. The executive power shall be vested in a president of the United States of America. He shall hold his office during the term of four years, and, together with the vice-president, chosen for the same term, be elected as follows

Each state shall appoint, in such manner as the legislature thereof may direct, a number of electors, equal to the whole number of senators and representatives to which the state may be entitled in Congress: but no senator or representative, or person holding an office of trust or profit under the United States, shall be appointed an Elector

The electors shall meet in their respective states, and vote by ballot for two persons, of whom one at least shall not be an inhabitant of the same state with themselves. And they shall make a list of all the persons voted for, and of the number of votes for each; which list they shall sign and certify, and transmit sealed to the seat of the government, directed to the president of the senate. The president of the senate shall in the presence of the senate and house of representatives open all the certificates, and the votes shall then be counted. The person having the greatest number of votes shall be the president, if such number be a majority of the whole number of electors appointed; and if there be more than one who have such majority, and have an equal number of votes, then the house of representatives shall immediately chuse by ballot one of them for president; and if no person have a majority, then from the five highest on the list the said house shall in like manner choose the president. But in choosing the president, the votes shall be taken by states, the representation from each state having one vote. A quorum for this purpose shall consist of a member or members from two-thirds of the states, and a majority of all the states shall be necessary to a choice. In every case, after the choice of the president, the person having the greatest number of votes of the electors shall be the vice-president. But if there should remain two or more who have equal votes, the senate shall choose from them by ballot the vice-president.

The Congress may determine the time of chusing the electors, and the day on which they shall give their votes; shall be the same throughout the United States.

No person except a natural born citizen, or a citizen of the United States, at the time of the adoption of this constitution, shall be eligible to the office of president; neither shall any person be eligible to that office who shall not have attained to the age of thirty-five years, and been fourteen years a resident within the United States.

In case of the removal of the president from office, or of his death, resignation, or inability to discharge the powers and duties of the said office, the same shall devolve on the vice-president, and the Congress may by law provide for the case of removal, death, resignation or inability, both of the president and vice president, declaring what officer shall then act as president, and such officer shall act accordingly, until the disability be removed, or president shall be elected

The president shall, at stated times, receive for his services a compensation, which shall neither be encreased nor diminished during the period for which he shall have been elected.

Before he enter on the execution of his office, he shall take the following oath or affirmation: "I——, do solemnly swear (or affirm) that I will faithfully execute the office of president of the United States, and will to the best of my, preserve, protect and defend the constitution of the United States."

Sect. 2. The president shall be commander in chief of the army and navy of the United States, and of the militia of the several States; he may require the opinion, in writing, of the principal officer in each of the executive departments, upon any subject relating to the duties of their respective offices, and he shall have power to grant reprieves and pardons for offences against the United States, except in cases of impeachment.

He shall have power, by and with the advice and consent of the senate, to make treaties, provided two-thirds of the senators present concur; and he shall nominate, and by and with the advice and consent of the senate, shall appoint ambassadors, other public ministers and consuls, judges of the supreme court, and all other officers of the United States, whose appointments are not herein otherwise provided for, and which shall be established by law.

The president shall have power to fill up all vacancies that may happen during the recess of the senate, by granting commissions which shall expire at the end of their next session.

Sect. 3. He shall from time to time give to the Congress information of the state of the union, and recommend to their consideration such measures as he shall judge necessary and expedient: he may, on extraordinary occasions, convene both houses, or either of them, and in case of disagreement between them, with respect to the time of adjournment, he may adjourn them to such time as he shall think proper: he shall receive ambassadors and other public ministers: he shall take care that the laws be faithfully executed, and shall commission all the officers of the United States.

Sect. 4. The president, vice-president and all civil officers of the United States, shall be removed from office on impeachment for, and conviction of treason, bribery, or other high crimes and misdemeanors.

III.

Sect. 1. The judicial power of the United States, shall be vested in one supreme court, and in such inferior courts as the Congress may from time to time ordain and establish. The judges, both of the supreme and inferior courts, shall hold their offices during good behaviour, and shall, at stated times, receive for their services, a compensation, which shall not be diminished during their continuance in office.

Sect. 2. The judicial power shall extend to all cases, both in law and equity, arising under this constitution, the laws of the United States, and treaties made, or which shall be made, under their

Committee of Style report, printed by Claypoole and Dunlap.
Manuscript Division

In the final days of the convention, much of the task of rewriting the various clauses fell to Gouverneur Morris. The Committee of Style report, which was virtually the finished product, came from Morris's pen.

had been discussed once the committee took on its assignment, "but there was sufficient room for the talents and taste stamped by the author on the face of it." So Morris's latter-day boast that he was the penman of the Constitution has Madison's endorsement. The plain truth, of course, is that Morris with his legal training and flair for the proper word gave an elegant form to the work of more than fifty talented, hardworking delegates.

A printed copy of the report was ordered for their perusal, then a North Carolina delegate expressed concern because "no provision was yet made for juries in Civil cases." When Gorham argued that it was not possible to direct which cases ought to be settled in a court of equity or where a jury might be needed, Mason agreed that "jury cases cannot be specified." Then Mason threw his bombshell, or maybe it was only a damp squib.

A general principle laid down on this and some other points would be suffi-cient. He wished the plan had been prefaced with a Bill of Rights, & would second a Motion if made for the purpose. It would give great quiet to the people; and with the aid of the State declarations, a bill might be prepared in a few hours.

Gerry agreed with enthusiasm and made the requested motion, but Sherman dealt the idea a death blow when he said that the states already had declarations of rights "and being in force are sufficient."[41] Although Mason pleaded that the "Laws of the U.S. are to be paramount to State Bills of Rights," the impatient delegates rejected the motion. Even Mason's own Virginia delegation, which knew of Mason's role in drafting the Virginia Declaration of Rights, voted against him.

Mason was too powerful to be ignored for long. When he begged the delegates to amend the no-tax-on-exports clause, by allowing states to levy duties to cover the costs of inspections or storage, the convention gave its approval after Madison conceded the suggestion "would at least be harmless." That concession to Mason was the last made to the trio that would, five days later, refuse to sign the finished plan. The last two working days were full of suggestions, some half-baked and some maturely thought out, to make further changes. Madison wanted authoriza-tion for creating a national university, Gerry and young Pinckney wanted to add a kind of bill of rights piecemeal, and Mason was still upset at the possibilities of a northern-inspired navigation act. The majority was in no mood for more compro-mising, however, and as the Saturday session wound to a close Randolph perceived

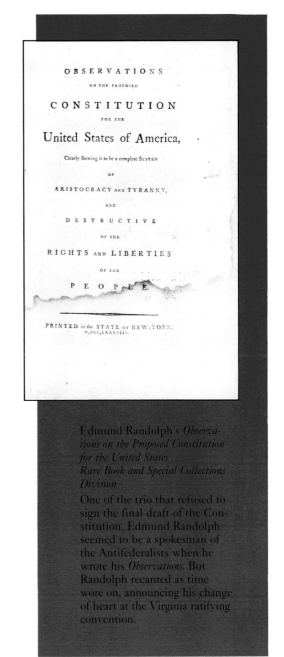

Edmund Randolph's *Observa-tions on the Proposed Constitution for the United States* . . . *Rare Book and Special Collections Division*
One of the trio that refused to sign the final draft of the Con-stitution, Edmund Randolph seemed to be a spokesman of the Antifederalists when he wrote his *Observations.* But Randolph recanted as time wore on, announcing his change of heart at the Virginia ratifying convention.

the tension. He chose the moment to fire his last bolt of dissent.

The delegates had overstepped their powers, Randolph began. He pleaded with the convention to follow his earlier advice, and allow a second convention to meet after the states debated the plan and made suggested amendments. If the delegates would not agree to his suggestion, Randolph said, it "would be impossible for him to put his name to the instrument." How much this disturbed Madison and Washington in the Virginia delegation we can only guess. But it gave courage to Mason, who was already thinking along the same line. As written, Mason warned, the plan "would end either in monarchy, or a tyrannical aristocracy." He joined Randolph in seeking a second convention. "It was improper to say to the people, take this or nothing." He would not sign the plan as it stood, but would add his name if the delegates included a second-convention proposal.

With the head of the largest delegation and another of its ablest members threatening to walk out, the convention diehards must have shaken their heads in distress. More worry was in store, as Gerry joined the dissenting Virginians with an explanation of why he would not sign. But all the delegations rejected a second-convention motion, and before adjourning for a Sunday recess a parchment copy of what everybody now called *the Constitution* was ordered. For those ready to sign, the ceremonies were set for Monday.

Engrossed copy of the Constitution of the United States, first page.
National Archives and Records Service

Doctor Franklin's *Bon Mot*

Benjamin Franklin. Portrait by Charles Willson Peale. *Photograph in the Prints and Photographs Division*

Benjamin Franklin's wisdom and common sense helped the delegates when an impasse developed, and at his suggestion the Constitution was made to appear the unanimous work of the convention. To the very last day, he encouraged a sense of moderation that triumphed when thirty-eight signers stepped forward on September 17.

During the sabbath break, some minds were set to thinking about the implications of what Gerry, Randolph, and Mason had threatened. Once the convention adjourned, the Constitution would be made public. How would it look if the state of Virginia or Massachusetts showed a split vote? And only Hamilton was present as the lone New York delegate. Wily Benjamin Franklin had a solution improvised when he rose to beseech all the delegates to sign. Franklin admitted he was not pleased with the whole document—but he had learned from long experience never to believe in his own infallibility. What about the plea for a second convention? Franklin demolished that notion. "I doubt too whether any other Convention we can obtain may be able to make a better Constitution." Any group of men will have a mixture of passions, errors, and selfish views. "From such an Assembly can a perfect production be expected?"

Franklin, the oldest delegate present, struck fellow delegate William Pierce as having "an activity of mind equal to a youth of 25 years of age." Perhaps Pierce remembered that youthful exuberance when Franklin made this last speech. America's enemies awaited word from their convention that would confirm the worst, Franklin said, "that our States are on the point of separation, only to meet hereafter for the purpose of cutting one another's throats."[42] He would sign the Constitution because he thought nothing better could be expected "and because I am not sure, that it is not the best." Everyone present should sign it, Franklin said, but to make sure that the world would receive an impression of near-unanimity he moved that the signing recognize the Constitution as approved "by the unanimous consent of *the States* present." The sly old gentleman had figured out a way for Hamilton to sign and make even absent New Yorkers a party to their business.

And so the convention came down to one last gesture of compromise. To dissent at this stage took either excessive stubbornness or enormous strength of character. Randolph apologized for not signing and predicted that nine states would not ratify. Gouverneur Morris made a last-minute plea to the three dissenters to remember they were only saying "that the *States* present were unanimous." Franklin protested that he had not made his proposal to entrap Randolph or any other delegate but had only hoped to prevent any mischief that might befall a delegate owing to "the refusal of his name."

No matter, the other delegates reasoned, for they were running out of patience. Respect for Washington caused a brief delay, as the delegates signified a willingness to give Washington his due and then be done with the business. As the last minutes of the convention ticked away, Washington made his first and only convention speech. When the general asked that the representation for each seat in the House be proportioned on thirty rather than forty thousand inhabitants, not a breath of opposition was heard.

What Gerry, Mason, and Randolph did next is of no importance, for thirty-eight delegates took the quill to affix their signatures. (John Dickinson, infirm and exhausted, had departed a few days earlier but not until George Read promised to sign for him.) As the signing proceeded, Franklin observed within Madison's hearing that he had often looked at the sun (carved on the president's chair) during their debates without deciding whether it was a sunrise or a sunset. Indeed, "Painters had found it difficult to distinguish in their art a rising from a setting sun. . . . But now at length I have the happiness to know that it is a rising and not a setting sun."[43]

Franklin's *bon mot* in the final moments of the convention probably gave a lilt to the proceedings, lifting the pall that descended after Randolph's last speech. Off the delegates trudged to the City Tavern where (Washington noted in his diary) they dined "and took a cordial leave of each other." Washington then returned to Robert Morris's house, where he had been a guest throughout the convention, and accepted the papers accumulated by Secretary William Jackson for safekeeping. Finally, it was time to be alone, and Washington reflected "on the momentous w[or]k which had been executed . . . for more than four months."[44]

Thus the convention ended on a quiet note. Printed copies of the Constitution were ordered for every delegate's use and more were dispatched via stagecoach to the congressmen waiting in New York. After months of secrecy, the Constitution was suddenly the nation's main conversational topic. Within a matter of days the entire document appeared in the *Pennsylvania Packet, and Daily Advertiser,* and by the end of October newspaper readers in every state were offered the full text. In short order the nation was inundated with the printed text, which was deceptively brief and gave no hint of the bargaining, heated debate, or close calls that sometimes left the next day's session problematical. The convention itself, drawing on the best minds in America, had become a kind of crucible for the republic. If all that heat and light produced anything, surely the product deserved a public hearing. If this was the best plan of government those "demi-gods" could offer, what might happen if the people rejected it was too distressing to contemplate.

In time every American newspaper would publish the complete text of the Constitution. The *Pennsylvania Packet, and Daily Advertiser* was first because it was printed by Claypoole & Dunlap, which had been printing the drafts all along. Sessions of the convention had been held in secret, but with the work over every citizen could read the document their representatives had produced "in order to form a more perfect union."

An unexpected sour note was sounded publicly almost at once. Mason had written some of his objections to the Constitution on his printed committee report, and he allowed friends in Philadelphia to copy them before he departed for Virginia. "There is no Declaration of Rights," it began, and might have stopped there; for no criticism of the Constitution carried more weight in the months ahead. The statement became a rallying point for adamant, moderate, and lukewarm opponents of the Constitution (who were soon lumped under the rubric of "Antifederalists"),

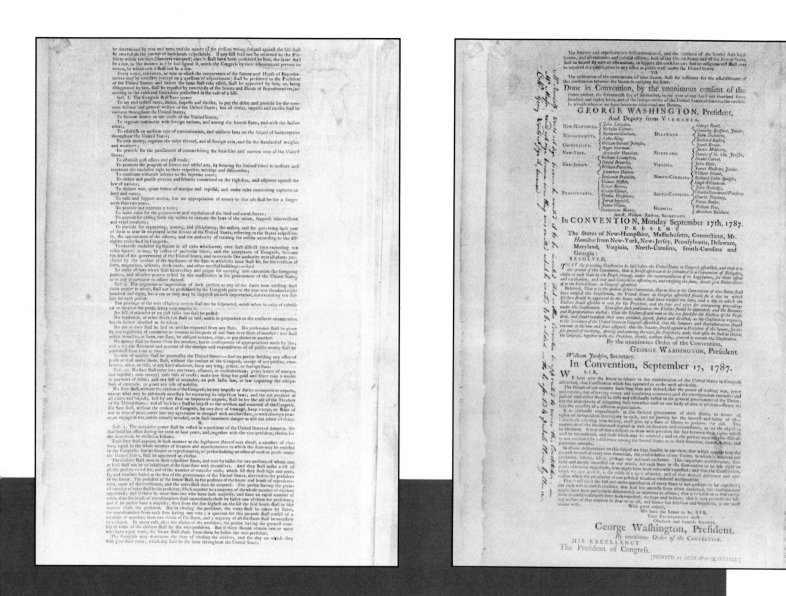

and overshadowed the rest of Mason's long critique of the powers of the Senate, president, and supreme court. Mason's *Objections* appeared in pamphlet form within days, telling the world what the nonsigner had said (almost word for word) on the convention floor.[45] The rapid circulation of Mason's dissent gave a signal to well-wishers of the Constitution. They must bestir themselves at once, to make sure that all the goodwill created by the first news from the convention would lead to a groundswell of favorable public opinion.

George Mason's "Objections to the Constitution . . .," October 7, 1787.
Manuscript Division

Virginia delegate George Mason grew more critical of the emerging Constitution, and when the work was in its last stages he wrote a series of objections. Hastily reprinted by other dissidents, Mason's *Objections* were broadcast by Antifederalists across the thirteen states and formed the basis for demands that a bill of rights be appended to the final draft.

No delegate felt this sense of urgency more acutely than James Madison. Alone of the Virginia delegates he headed northward, returning to his post in the Continental Congress. There he soon perceived he was not surrounded by admirers of the proposed Constitution. Richard Henry Lee, also a Virginia delegate, was Patrick Henry's friend and like Henry declined serving at the convention, but he had visited Philadelphia while it was under way and knew what was taking shape. "Being a Member of Congress," Lee told John Adams, "where the plan of Convention must be approved, there appeared an inconsistency for Members of the former to have Session with the latter, and so pass judgment at New York upon their opinion at Philadelphia."[46] Lee was suspicious by nature, and his correspondence with Mason confirmed a dislike for the final shape of the Constitution.

When Congress received the Constitution thousands of Americans had already read its text. Word for word, line for line, the Constitution hatched in secrecy was now made available for the fullest public discussion. Nothing like this had ever happened before, and perhaps never will again, for as congressmen began to consider the merits of the new plan thousands of clergymen, farmers, lawyers, shopkeepers, doctors, blacksmiths, and merchants were reading it themselves. In this atmosphere, the power of a covering letter signed by the revered Washington was evident. Although penned by Morris, the letter seemed an unqualified endorsement of the Constitution by Washington. That was Morris's intention, of course, but it gave the Constitution a head start that the opposition never overcame.

But the Antifederalists did not give up easily. In Congress, Lee tried to derail any hurried attempt to ratify the Constitution. As Madison explained to Jefferson,

> When the plan came before Congs. for their sanction, a very serious effect was made by R. H. Lee & Mr. Dane of Masts. to embarrass it. It was first contended that Congress could not properly give any positive countenance to a measure which had for its object the subversion of the Constitution under which they acted. This ground of attack failing, the former gentleman urged the expediency of sending out the plan with amendments, & proposed a number of them corresponding with the objections of Col. Mason. This experiment had still less effect. In order however to obtain unanimity it was necesssary to couch the resolution [of transmittal to the states] in very moderate terms.[47]

Lee had a different version. "It was with us, as with you," he wrote Mason, "this or nothing; and this urged with the most extreme intemperance. The greatness of the

Richard Henry Lee of Virginia did not serve at Philadelphia during the convention, but he visited the city while debates were in progress and concluded that the states were being cheated of their rights by the new document. In league with Patrick Henry and George Mason, Lee tried to prevent outright ratification of the Constitution and was rewarded by Henry with a seat in the first Federal Senate in 1789.

John Jay. From Du Simitiere, *Portraits of the Generals*, 1783. *Rare Book and Special Collections Division*

John Jay of New York did not attend the Philadelphia convention, but he was active in supporting the ratification movement. He joined Hamilton and Madison in preparing the *Federalist* essays until illness forced him to the sidelines.

powers given, and the multitude of places to be created produce a coalition of monarchy men, military men, aristrocrats and drones, whose noise, impudence and zeal exceeds all belief."[48] The states below the Potomac would suffer greatly under the new plan, Lee added. "The commercial plunder of the South stimulates the rapacious trader. In this state of things the patriot voice is raised in vain."

Whether in vain or not, Lee busied himself to spread seeds of discord. "I find it impossible for me to doubt, that in its present State, unamended," Lee wrote a friend, ratification of the Constitution "will put Civil Liberty and the happiness of the people at the mercy of Rulers who may possess the great unguarded powers given."[49] Lee and other Antifederalists leaders adopted the tactics of delay, hoping to win converts to the idea that a second convention was needed to correct the imperfections written into the Constitution by the first gathering. A call for a second convention and the complaint that the Constitution lacked a bill of rights was all they had, and with most of the country's ninety-eight or so newspapers working against them, their task was not an easy one. Never a well-organized group, the Antifederalists adopted a piecemeal strategy calling for amendment of the Constitution before final ratification. To slow down the Federalists in states where the Antifederalists controlled the state legislatures, they set distant dates for ratification conventions. New York, Virginia, and North Carolina scheduled theirs for the summer of 1788 in a mixed gesture of indifference and defiance.

Where the pro-Constitution party (soon called "Federalists") held power, they brooked no delay. Delaware hurriedly called a convention and became the first ratifying state in early December. Within a week, Pennsylvania joined her smaller sister state, though not without some skirmishing and protesting from western delegates that "indecent haste" robbed the people of an opportunity to consider the Constitution on its merits. Six days later, New Jersey became the third ratifying state. Reports that Georgia ratified on January 2, 1788, were soon confirmed in newspapers favoring the Constitution. "The fourth grand pillar is erected," the Federalist press trumpeted.

To Madison, the reports of quick victories and predictions of swift tidings from the necessary nine conventions looked a little too easy. To counter the apparent Antifederalist scheme of a propaganda barrage designed to bring the ratification process to a halt, Madison agreed to Hamilton's proposal that they join with John Jay to write a series of newspaper essays that would appeal to thinking people in

New York. Written over the pen name of "Publius," their explanations and urgings would become a famous treatise titled *The Federalist;* but at the time they drew from a French commentator the observation that "they were too learned for the average man."[49] Madison stayed at his New York listening post, eager for news from Massachusetts, where a battle took shape that disquieted friends of the Constitution. For the first time, the new plan had been thoroughly debated at town meetings and at first glance it seemed that men instructed to vote against the Constitution might outnumber its friends. "Our prospects are gloomy, but hope is not entirely extinguished," Rufus King wrote Madison. As in Philadelphia, some concessions might be needed, for there was much criticism concerning the lack of a bill of rights. "We are now thinking of Amendments to be submitted not as a condition of our assent & ratification, but as the Opinion of the Convention subjoined to their ratification. This scheme may gain a few members but the issue is doubtful."[50] Madison sent this pessimistic report on to Washington, with the comment that perhaps King was unduly cautious.

In fact, King was telling Madison the bad news in case it grew worse. For to have Massachusetts ratify the Constitution conditionally, as the Antifederalists urged, would have jeopardized the whole process. An adverse vote at the Boston convention would not only throw off the Federalists' timetable, but also encourage the known dissidents in New England to exert themselves. Hence the Federalists used every device short of bribery to see that the Constitution was neither rejected nor conditionally ratified. At first Governor Hancock stood aloof from the proceedings, making Antifederalists suspicious. "Hancock pretends to be sick," Richard Henry Lee was told. After conferring with friends of the Constitution, however, Hancock experienced a miraculous recovery and suddenly appeared at the convention carrying a set of amendments. The sought-after amendments amounted to a bill of rights plus a list of Antifederalist objections, and purportedly came from Hancock's pen. With the old patriot's imprimatur, these were approved as "recommendatory amendments" and the Constitution ratified by a narrow margin. The sighs of relief in Federalist circles probably were loud enough to be heard across the Charles River in Cambridge, but the point was that Massachusetts ratified (187 to 168) on February 6, 1788.

From the day Madison learned of the Boston convention outcome he breathed much easier. "The amendments are a blemish, but are in the least Offensive form," he wrote Washington. "The minority also is very disagreeably large, but the temper of it is some atonement. I am assured by Mr. King that the leaders of it as well as the members of it in general are in good humour; and will countenance no irregular opposition there or elsewhere."[51] In other words, once a state ratified there would be no more talk about second conventions or further meetings to try to incorporate a bill of rights into the original document.

Discouraged by the Boston event, Antifederalists looked to the remaining conventions in New Hampshire and the South for some signs of genuine resistance. Then word from Rhode Island electrified some citizens and angered others. From Providence the news was unusual, in that the legislature had submitted the Constitution directly to the people—a one-man, one-vote proposition allowing each freeholder to place his aye or nay on the Constitution. Sensing defeat, the Federalists had urged a boycott of the election, so that the total vote determined 237 ballots favoring the Constitution, 2,708 against it. Antifederalists elsewhere were bewildered, not knowing whether to exult in the results of a direct election or to concede that the small state was usually on the wrong side of most public questions. An angry Boston Federalist suggested that a bit of roughing up and saber-rattling might bring the Rhode Islanders to their senses. Nowhere else was such an experiment in direct democracy encouraged.

"The Sacred Fire of Liberty"

"Liberty. In the form of the Goddess of Youth giving Support to the Bald Eagle."
Prints and Photographs Division

An emotional outburst followed the first announcement of the completed Constitution. This allegorical engraving, depicting the Goddess of Youth in the form of a young woman, symbolized the feeling that America was about to launch a great venture among the nations of the world.

Jefferson and John Adams read the trans-Atlantic mails and their American newspapers with unusual interest with the coming of winter in 1787. They exchanged letters with comments on the proposed Constitution and found themselves in agreement. "What think you of a Declaration of Rights?" Adams asked. "Should not such a Thing have preceeded the Model?" Jefferson agreed, and his republican instincts forced him to say that the president created by the Constitution "seems a bad edition of a Polish king."[52] Jefferson was equally frank in writing Madison his first impressions, listing first the constitutional features he liked (separation of powers, the taxing power in Congress), and then moving to "what I do not like. First the omission of a bill of rights."[53] To another Virginian, Jefferson suggested that the necessary nine states ought to ratify the Constitution while the last four held out for amendments. Silently, Madison must have wished Jefferson had not been such an indefatigible penman.

From his Paris watchtower Jefferson discerned correctly that much of the ratification burden fell on Madison's shoulders. To an American diplomat in Spain Jefferson reported the Constitution was running into difficulty. "Madison will be it's main pillar: but tho an immensely powerful one, it is questionable whether he can bear the weight of such a host. So that the presumption is that Virginia will reject it."[54]

Jefferson's guess was based on more than the known hostility of Patrick Henry toward the Constitution. Henry, the dominant figure in Virginia courthouse politics, heard of the reaction by Lee and Mason and that was good enough for him. To intimates Henry said he had not gone to Philadelphia because "he smelt a rat," and the clear message was that these three would join Governor Randolph to stop the ratification steamroller. At Henry's bidding the Virginia legislature provided for a ratifying convention in June, clearly committed to demanding a second convention as their ultimatum to Federalists. The Antifederalists also insisted on a series of forty amendments covering both a bill of rights and bulwarks to protect southern planters in the world commodity markets from northern exploitation. Moreover, Henry sent out messages to North Carolina, urging their sister state to stand with Virginia Antifederalists. Willie Jones, who was as close to being a political boss as North Carolina had, readily agreed to the proposition. George Clinton thought the Virginia propositions deserved full support.

Madison hoped to avoid a trip home that spring and would have stayed in New York if the Virginia ratifying convention looked safe for the Federalists. His friends warned him, however, that without his presence the Lee-Henry-Mason forces (presumably joined by Randolph) would overwhelm the Federalists. Reluctantly, Madison came to Richmond and began counting heads. Two quick developments changed the complexion of the convention. Randolph, after hemming-and-hawing his way through the winter, revealed he had switched positions. Now he favored outright ratification. This stunned Mason, who called his former friend a Judas and girded for a longer convention than was first expected. The other less obvious move favoring the Federalists was the effect Washington's name had on delegates. How could any loyal Virginian vote against something Washington favored?

Before that final tally, there were days when Henry seemed to be in command. Nobody in Virginia could match the old spellbinder when Henry took a dip of snuff and started ripping into the opposition. But in Richmond that summer Henry met his match. John Marshall, who served as a Federalist delegate, recalled that for logic and skill Madison was unequaled as he took Henry's rambling remarks, often baited with racial slurs or petty snipings, and turned them into Antifederalist liabilities. The Antifederalists hoped to delay a vote, knowing that New Yorkers were holding their convention in Poughkeepsie at the same time. If they both stopped short of outright ratification, the New York-Virginia alliance might force the Federalists into drastic concessions. The strategy backfired. Henry wanted a clause-for-clause debate and got it, only to abandon the logic of such a scheme by a series of weak digressions. Mason, so masterful in debate at Philadelphia, proved nearly as inept as Henry when the Federalists called them to account.

Patrick Henry. Engraving published by James Webster.
Prints and Photographs Division
The famous Virginia orator led the opposition to the Constitution in his state on the grounds that it endangered both state and individual liberties.

Abraham Yates. Etching by
Max Rosenthal.
Prints and Photographs Division

Antifederalist Abraham Yates
believed that New York should
oppose the new Constitution
"even if all the twelve states
were to come in" for it.

For the Antifederalists, matters moved from bad to worse, but Madison saw no signs of a collapse in their overall strategy. Hamilton, serving in the New York convention, authorized an express rider to carry any good news northward from Richmond. To his New York friend Madison sent a glimmer of hope. "A few days more will probably produce a decision; though it is surmised that something is expected from your Convention," Madison reported (the Henry-Mason-Clinton link was an open secret). "At present It is calculated that we still retain a majority of 3 or 4; and if we can weather the storm agst. the part under consideration I shall hold the danger to be pretty well over."[55] If the Federalists lost, Madison reasoned, the blame would fall on the Kentucky district delegates.

Madison was a dedicated worrier. He had left the Philadelphia convention with mixed feelings, convinced that because his favored scheme of a legislative veto on state laws had been scrapped the Constitution might not work. He fretted when the Pennsylvania opposition cried foul and stirred up a fuss in the newspapers. The close vote at Boston alarmed him, and when New Hampshire's convention adjourned without ratifying, Madison was even more concerned. But by late June Madison perceived all the work of the past two years was coming to a successful conclusion. After Henry made a hysterical speech, full of bugbears about old debts to British merchants, freed slaves, and "trial by jury gone," Madison realized that they were headed for victory. He told Washington that Mason betrayed a mood of utter hopelessness. "Col. Mason . . . talked in a style which no other sentiment could have produced."[56]

Henry's last gasp was an attempt to shunt aside an unqualified ratification of the Constitution in favor of resolutions calling for "previous amendments." Theoretically, if the resolution passed, Virginia would not be a full member of the Union unless her list of amendments gained acceptance. Anxiously the tellers counted. Madison had miscalculated, but no matter, for the shifting of votes hurt Antifederalists. The Kentucky delegates stuck with Henry, but those from the region between the Shenandoah Valley and the upper Ohio voted with the Federalists. Eighty-eight nays turned back the eighty aye votes. Henry had lost. The Constitution was saved.

A jubilant Madison sent the express rider scurrying northward to the New York ratifying convention in Poughkeepsie. His joy would have been greater had he known that New Hampshire had reconvened its convention and ratified five days earlier with an eleven-vote majority. When Madison wrote his message, the express rider from Concord was already resting his horse in a Poughkeepsie stable, having brought the news from New Hampshire as instructed by Federalists more than eager to pay his bill. But, the New York Antifederalists were determined to play their role to the end. Sour-faced Abraham Yates heard the report from Concord at his post in the Continental Congress. Asked what this development meant to the Poughkeepsie delegates, Yates vowed his friends there would act "the same [as] they would have done if New Hampshire had not adopted" the Constitution. In spite of the pressure, Yates was convined "that if all the twelve States were to come in that New York ought not and I trusted they would not."[57]

Yates knew his friends well. The New York Antifederalists brushed aside the New Hampshire news. Melancton Smith shrugged and declared he had always expected nine states would ratify the Constitution anyway. Perhaps Clinton's allies were bluffing, in that they plainly expected more cooperation from fellow Antifederalists in Virginia. At the outset, Governor George Clinton must have counted on a twenty-vote majority.[58] With that kind of pressure on Federalists, the Clintonians calculated they could work out an arrangement with the Virginia Antifederalists.

A jointly issued ultimatum was their initial strategy, but this depended on comfortable majorities in Richmond and Poughkeepsie (as once seemed the case). Contrary to early expectations, the Virginia Antifederalists could not deliver on the promises. New York was isolated. The second time around, New Hampshire ratified without any qualifications, as had Virginia. Either the New York Antifederalists could admit the game was over, or they could ignore the results in other states and pursue an indifferent, Rhode Island-like policy.

The shock from Richmond was only mildly felt in Poughkeepsie on July 2, however, when the Virginia result was announced by William Livingston. The Antifederalists let their opponents cheer, then went about their business and proceeded to talk and vote as though nothing had happened to prevent a conditional ratification. "We are debating on amendments without deciding what is to be done with them," a frustrated Hamilton told Madison.[59]

Federalists on Manhattan heard of these delays with disgust. Robert R. Livingston warned the New York convention that if they failed to ratify the Constitution a secessionist movement could materialize downriver. Hamilton told Madison a few

George Clinton. Engraving by P. Maverick after a painting by Ames.
Prints and Photographs Division

New York governor George Clinton was unwilling to surrender his own power or any part of the state's sovereignty, and he worked with Antifederalist forces to prevent ratification.

69

weeks earlier that the Antifederalists would try to drag their feet as long as they could, and would even ignore a threat of "A separation of the Southern district from the other part of the state." In short, Hamilton predicted, Clinton's strategy—despite hell, high water, or ratification by nine states—was to stall for time.[60]

His accurate prophecy meant that any threat from Manhattan might backfire, but as a spokesman for the New York merchant community, Hamilton had nothing to lose when he insisted that "a separation would . . . inevitably take place if New York rejected the Constitution."[61] Governor Clinton bristled, but his twenty-vote majority had melted away. All hope of cooperation with the Virginia Antifederalists seemed chimerical. Even the flinty Yates was ready to give up. "Can our State stand alone?" he asked another Clintonian. "Is our State wiser than all the Rest &ca." Even "if that storm [of Virginia ratification] is wethered I suppose they will see that it will be in vain to throw any farther Obstecles in the way and they will soon finish" at Poughkeepsie.[62]

Thus the war of nerves between the contending forces at Poughkeepsie wound to a climax. Hamilton began talking with more confidence, the Antifederalists started each day a bit more subdued, and finally on July 23 all the starch was gone from the Clintonian banners. A resolution to send along a bill of rights and other amendments as a condition for ratification was proposed as a desperate measure, but the Federalists insisted this was improper and unacceptable. Hamilton read a letter from Madison in which the Virginian said a ratification based on conditions would prevent New York from becoming "a member of the New Union, and consequently . . . she could not be received into the plan." The Constitution, Madison added, "requires an adoption *in toto*, and *for ever*."[63] The impasse was broken when an Antifederalist moved that the conditional wording be changed to say New York ratified "in full confidence" that its recommended amendments would receive "an early and mature Consideration." Clinton kept his silence. Twelve Antifederalists deserted their leader to give the amended resolution a two-vote majority. New York was not leaving the Union after all.

In their victory the New York Federalists were overly magnanimous. They left enough room in a string of recommended amendments for the Antifederalists to claim they had not lost the battle—twenty-three "explanatory" amendments were followed by thirty-two "recommendatory" articles. Further salve for their con-

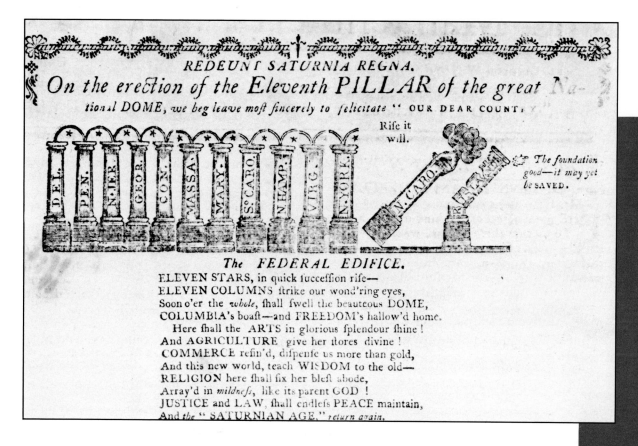

REDEUNT SATURNIA REGNA.

On the erection of the Eleventh PILLAR of the great National DOME, we beg leave most sincerely to felicitate " OUR DEAR COUNTRY."

Rise it will.

The foundation good—it may yet be SAVED.

The FEDERAL EDIFICE.

ELEVEN STARS, in quick succession rise—
ELEVEN COLUMNS strike our wond'ring eyes,
Soon o'er the *whole*, shall swell the beauteous DOME,
COLUMBIA's boast—and FREEDOM's hallow'd home.
 Here shall the ARTS in glorious splendour shine !
And AGRICULTURE give her stores divine !
COMMERCE refin'd, dispense us more than gold,
And this new world, teach WISDOM to the old—
RELIGION here shall fix her blest abode,
Array'd in *mildness*, like its parent GOD !
JUSTICE and LAW, shall endless PEACE maintain,
And *the* " SATURNIAN AGE," return again.

sciences came in a letter, written by John Jay, which was to circulate in all the states calling for a second general convention.

Madison's joy upon hearing of the New York ratification was diluted when he saw the circular letter. All the Federalist strategy would be undone by a second convention, Madison reasoned, for the letter "has given fresh hopes and exertions to those who opposed the Constitution."[64] The Antifederalists, he wrote Jefferson, would now seek "an early Convention composed of men who will essentially mutilate the system. . . . An early Convention is in every view to be dreaded in the present temper of America. A very short period of delay would produce the double advantage of diminishing the heat and increasing the light of all parties."

Coinciding with the report from Poughkeepsie was a message from North Carolina. Antifederalists in Hillsboro out-Henryed the Virginia Antifederalists by placing the Constitution on hold—they voted neither to reject nor ratify—but expected another convention to be held. Then, responding to the New York circular letter, the North Carolina legislature authorized five delegates to attend the proposed second convention. Embarrassed Federalists fumed. "Was this a time to smoak a pipe, & suck the paw like a surly Bear, when your house was on fire?"[65]

Willie Jones proved to be a better convention manager than Patrick Henry, but the gesture was part of a sham battle. The real fight was over. Parades in Philadelphia, New York, and other Federalist strongholds provided an outlet for public exuberance and gave rise to expectations that Congress would establish the new government with swift strokes. Elections for Congress were authorized in the eleven ratifying states, and plans for an electoral college to choose a president proceeded. Washington's name was on every tongue as citizens repeated what had been said so many times during the ratification struggle: "Washington will be the first president. Nothing can go wrong with Washington at the helm."

Rarely in history has one man been so completely trusted as George Washington. Rarer still is the man deserving of that trust. But with hindsight the role Washington played in bringing about the Philadelphia convention, in serving as the nominal presiding officer, and in sending the finished product off to the states (with a laudatory covering letter) made final acceptance of the Constitution most likely. Although frustrated Antifederalists decried the power of Washington's endorsement, they had no public figure of comparable stature to challenge the great man's implied approval. The unanimous vote for Washington in the first electoral college proved the truth of earlier predictions that the commander-in-chief of 1776 would never desert his country in a time of great stress. Such had been the deciding argument during the Virginia ratifying convention, as Jefferson learned at his French listening-post. "Be assured," Monroe wrote, Washington's "influence carried this government."[66] By October 1788 Madison laid all the rumors to rest, when he told Jefferson: "There is no doubt that Genl. Washington will be called to the Presidency."[67]

At last Madison began to feel the Constitution had a chance. His earlier reservations were dropped as he started to think about his own role in the new government. There were promises to keep, solemnly made on the campaign trail and in Richmond, to add amendments that would reassure citizens that a bill of rights would soon be part of "the supreme law of the land." Scores of other delegates at the Philadelphia convention found themselves in similar circumstances. By the natural order of things, when the first Congress assembled in New York the following spring eight signers of the Constitution filled eight of twenty-two Senate seats. In the first House of Representatives Madison was joined by Gerry, Sherman, and Williamson. The new government abounded with constitution-makers!

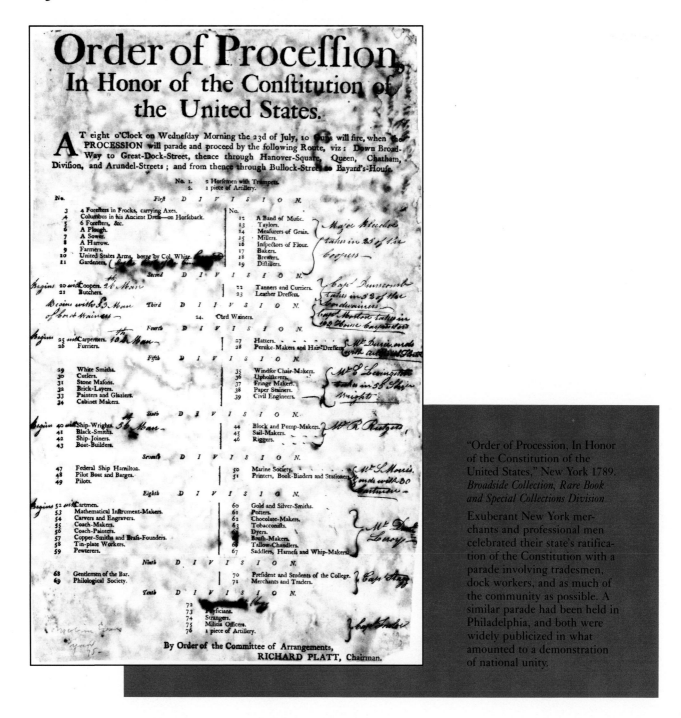

"Order of Procession, In Honor of the Constitution of the United States," New York 1789. *Broadside Collection, Rare Book and Special Collections Division*

Exuberant New York merchants and professional men celebrated their state's ratification of the Constitution with a parade involving tradesmen, dock workers, and as much of the community as possible. A similar parade had been held in Philadelphia, and both were widely publicized in what amounted to a demonstration of national unity.

When Washington was inaugurated on April 30, 1789, he recalled the events which had first brought him the public's confidence. Every man involved in the Revolution then harbored some doubts about the outcome. Their lives were committed to the proposition that the Revolution had been a blessing for America and the world. Moreover, recent experience proved that America could never rest, but must be involved in the business of overcoming adversity. Eighteen months earlier, Washington's resolve firmed as he read of the Shays uprising. Perhaps that "little rebellion" had been a disguised blessing, considering the country's response. None of these things needed to be said, however, as Washington prepared to take the presidential oath. What mattered was that the Union forged in 1776 had survived its first peacetime test. "The preservation of the sacred fire of liberty, and the destiny of the Republican model of Government," Washington said, "are justly considered as *deeply*, perhaps *finally* staked, on the experiment entrusted to the hands of the American people."[68]

Liberty and self-government—the twin goals of the American Revolution—were the legacy Washington wanted his country to bequeath to all mankind. The risk-takers of 1787 decided it was time once again to show the world that their Revolution had permanently affected men everywhere. Their solution was embodied in the Constitution. Two hundred years later, a nation sustained by an abiding faith in that Constitution continues the experiment.

Notes

1. John C. Fitzpatrick, ed., *The Writings of Washington*, 39 vols. (Washington: U.S. Government Printing Office, 1931-44), 26:486, 29:34.

2. Elbridge Gerry to Rufus King, November 29, 1786. Charles R. King, ed. *Life and Correspondence of Rufus King*, 6 vols. (New York: G. P. Putnam's Sons, 1894-1900), 1:197.

3. N. C. Ford et al., eds., *Journals of the Continental Congress*, 34 vols. (Washington: U.S. Government Printing Office, 1905-37), 30:87-88.

4. William T. Hutchinson and William M. E. Rachal (vols. 1-7) and Robert A. Rutland et al. (vols. 8-) eds., *The Papers of James Madison* (Chicago: University of Chicago Press, 1962-77; Charlottesville: University Press of Virginia, 1978-), 9:187.

5. Fitzpatrick, *Writings of Washington*, 29:122.

6. Hutchinson, *Madison Papers*, 9:199.

7. Ibid. 9:285.

8. Ibid. 9:362.

9. Edmund C. Burnett, ed., *Letters of Members of the Continental Congress*, 8 vols. (Washington: Carnegie Institution of Washington, 1921-36), 8:572, 581.

10. Robert A. Rutland, ed., *The Papers of George Mason*, 3 vols. (Chapel Hill: University of North Carolina Press, 1970), 3:879-80.

11. Lester J. Cappon, ed., *The Adams-Jefferson Letters*, 2 vols. (Chapel Hill: University of North Carolina Press, 1959), 1:196.

12. Rutland, *Mason Papers*, 3:892-3.

13. Max Farrand, ed., *The Records of the Federal Convention*, 4 vols. (1911-37; reprint, New Haven, Conn.: Yale University Press, 1966), 1:30.

14. Cappon, *Adams-Jefferson*, 1:196.

15. Rutland, *Mason Papers*, 3:893.

16. Farrand, *Records*, 3:479.

17. Ibid. 1:164, 175.

18. Ibid. 3:91.

19. Ibid. 1:288.

20. Ibid. 3:94.

21. Ibid. 1:451.

22. Ibid. 2:17-18.

23. Ibid. 1:511.

24. Hutchinson, *Madison Papers*, 10:105.

25. Farrand, *Records*, 2:3.

26. Ibid. 1:168.

27. Clinton Rossiter, *1787: The Grand Convention* (New York: Macmillan, 1966), 197.

28. Hutchinson, *Madison Papers*, 10:240.

29. Farrand, *Records*, 1:486, 592.

30. Ibid. 2:95.

31. Ibid. 2:183, 415.

32. Ibid. 2:370; Ibid. 2:499*n*, 450.

33. Rossiter, *1787: The Grand Convention*, 212.

34. Farrand, *Records*, 2:377, 412-4.

35. Ibid. 2:344.

36. Ibid. 2:529-30.

37. Ibid. 2:522.

38. Ibid. 2:556.

39. Ibid. 2:560-61.

40. Ibid. 3:499.

41. Ibid. 2:587-8.

42. Ibid. 2:642-3.

43. Ibid. 2:648.

44. John C. Fitzpatrick, ed., *The Diaries of George Washington 1748-1799*, 4 vols. (Boston: Houghton Mifflin, 1925), 3:237.

45. Rutland, *Mason Papers*, 3:991-93.

46. J. C. Ballagh, ed., *The Letters of Richard Henry Lee*, 2 vols. (New York: Macmillan 1911-1914), 2:434.

47. Hutchinson, *Madison Papers*, 10:217.

48. Ballagh, *Lee Letters*, 2:438.

49. Robert A. Rutland, *Ordeal of the Constitution: The Antifederalists and the Ratification Struggle of 1787-1788* (Norman, Okla.: University of Oklahoma Press, 1966), 137-8.

50. Hutchinson, *Madison Papers*, 10:455.

51. Ibid. 10:510.

52. Cappon, *Adams-Jefferson*, 1:210-2.

53. Hutchinson, *Madison Papers*, 10:336.

54. Julian P. Boyd et al., eds., *The Papers of Thomas Jefferson*, 21 vols. to date (Princeton, N.J.: Princeton University Press, 1950-), 12:425.

55. Hutchinson, *Madison Papers*, 11:157.

56. Ibid. 11:168.

57. Linda Grant De Pauw, *The Eleventh Pillar: New York State and the Federal Constitution* (Ithaca, N.Y.: Cornell University Press, 1966), 208.

58. Ibid. 184.

59. Hutchinson, *Madison Papers*, 11:192.

60. Ibid. 11:99.

61. De Pauw, *The Eleventh Pillar*, 231.

62. Abraham Yates to Robert Lansing, June 29, 1788. Yates Papers, New York Public Library.

63. Hutchinson, *Madison Papers*, 11:189.

64. Ibid. 11:238.

65. Robert A. Rutland, *The Birth of the Bill of Rights 1776-1791* (Boston: Northeastern University Press, 1983), 187.

66. Rutland, *Ordeal of the Constitution*, 253.

67. Hutchinson, *Madison Papers*, 11:276.

68. Fitzpatrick, *Writings of Washington*, 30:294-5.